CALIFORNIA DMV HANDBOOK

ACADEMIC TEST ACE PRESS

Introduction

Welcome to " The Ultimate California DMV Handbook." Whether you're a new driver eager to get behind the wheel or a seasoned driver looking to renew your license, this guide is designed to help you navigate the process smoothly and confidently. The California DMV exam is a critical step in ensuring that all drivers on the road are knowledgeable and safe, and passing it is a milestone in your driving journey.

The purpose of this guide is to provide you with the most up-to-date and comprehensive preparation for the California DMV exam. It combines extensive knowledge of traffic laws, road signs, and safe driving practices with practical tips and techniques to help you succeed. By breaking down the test into manageable sections and offering real, essential information, this guide aims to demystify the exam and boost your confidence.

With detailed chapters on everything from scheduling your exam to mastering safe driving practices, this guide ensures you have all the tools you need to pass the California DMV exam with flying colors. Get ready to embark on your driving journey with confidence and knowledge, equipped with the best preparation available.

As a bonus, we've created detailed flashcards to help reinforce your learning. At the end of this book, you will find a link or QR code to scan, which will lead you to the flashcards for easy downloading. After you've completed this guide and taken your exam, we would greatly appreciate your honest review. Your feedback is invaluable in helping us enhance our materials and ensure future readers have the best possible resources.

Please scan the QR code below if you'd like to leave a review.

Thank you for your support!

Chapter I: Understanding the California DMV Exam

How to Schedule Your Exam

1. Create an account on the California DMV website (dmv.ca.gov).
2. Complete the online application (DL 44 form).
3. Choose a convenient DMV office location.
4. Select an available date and time for your exam.
5. Pay the required fees.

Tip: Schedule your exam well in advance, as appointment slots can fill up quickly, especially in urban areas.

The Testing Process: Driver's License Tests

This chapter provides a comprehensive overview of the tests required to obtain a driver's license in California.

1. Vision Test

All applicants must pass a vision test to ensure they can see well enough to drive safely. If you take the vision test with corrective lenses or contact lenses, your driver's license will indicate this restriction. If you fail the vision test, you will need to have your eye doctor complete a Report of Vision Examination form. For more details, visit dmv.ca.gov/vision-standards.

2. Written Knowledge Test

This computer-based test, conducted at DMV offices, assesses your understanding of California traffic laws, road signs, and safe driving practices. The number of questions varies depending on the type of license:

- **Class C License:** Adults face a 36-question test, while teenage applicants have a 46-question test.
- **Scoring and Attempts:** You must correctly answer about 83% of the questions to pass (38 out of 46 for teenagers). Applicants are given three chances to pass the written test per application.

3. Behind-the-Wheel Drive Test

Applicants for an original driver's license must pass a behind-the-wheel test to demonstrate their ability to safely operate a vehicle. Drivers renewing their license may be required to take this test if they have a vision or medical condition. The practical exam evaluates your ability to safely operate a vehicle in real-world conditions. Conducted with a DMV examiner in your vehicle, the test lasts about 20 minutes. You start with a score of 100 points, losing points for any errors, and must maintain a score of 70 or higher to pass. During the test, the examiner may give two or more instructions at once to assess your ability to understand and follow directions, such as "At the next street, make a left turn, and then at the first intersection make another left turn."

To schedule your behind-the-wheel test, visit dmv.ca.gov/make-an-appointment.

Pre-Drive Inspection:

Before beginning the test, the DMV examiner will ask you to demonstrate the following:

- **Driver's Window:** The window on the driver's side must open.
- **Windshield:** Must provide a clear, unobstructed view for you and the examiner. Windshield cracks may delay your test.
- **Horn:** Must be in proper working condition and loud enough to be heard from at least 200 feet away.
- **Tires:** Must have at least 1/32-inch of uniform tread depth. Donut tires are not allowed during the test.
- **Rearview Mirrors:** At least two rearview mirrors are required, with one on the left side of the vehicle.
- **Foot Brake:** There must be at least one inch of clearance between the brake pedal and the floorboard when the brake is depressed.
- **Brake Lights:** Both left and right brake lights must be functional.
- **Emergency (Parking) Brake:** Must know how to set and release it.
- **Turn/Arm Signals:**
    - Left turn
    - Right turn
    - Slowing down or stopping
- **Windshield Wipers:** Must be able to show they function.
- **Seatbelts:** All seatbelts must work properly and be used by the individuals in the vehicle.

NOTE: If your vehicle does not meet these requirements, your drive test will be rescheduled.

Eligibility Requirements

To apply for a California driver's license, you must meet specific eligibility requirements. These requirements vary slightly based on the type of license you are applying for, such as a Class C (standard), Class M (motorcycle), or Commercial Driver's License (CDL). Below, we outline the general eligibility criteria for obtaining a driver's license in California.

Age Requirements

1. **Class C Driver's License:**
   o **Minimum Age:** You must be at least 16 years old to apply for a provisional Class C driver's license. However, you can apply for a learner's permit at 15½ years old.
   o **Adults (18 and older):** If you are 18 or older, you can apply for a regular Class C driver's license without needing a learner's permit first.
2. **Class M (Motorcycle) License:**
   o **Minimum Age:** You must be at least 16 years old to apply for a Class M1 or M2 motorcycle license. A learner's permit for motorcycles can be obtained at 15½ years old.
3. **Commercial Driver's License (CDL):**
   o **Minimum Age:** You must be at least 18 years old to drive within California (intrastate). To drive commercially across state lines (interstate), you must be at least 21 years old.

Documentation Needed

When applying for any type of driver's license, you must provide several forms of documentation to prove your identity, residency, and legal presence.

1. **Proof of Identity:** An original or certified copy of a U.S. birth certificate, U.S. passport, or permanent resident card (Green Card).
2. **Proof of Residency:** You need two documents to prove California residency, such as utility bills, rental or lease agreements, mortgage bills, or school documents. The documents must display your name and physical address.
3. **Proof of Legal Presence:** Non-U.S. citizens must provide documents that prove legal presence in the U.S., such as a work permit or an employment authorization card.
4. **Social Security Number (SSN):** You must provide your social security number. If you are ineligible for an SSN, you must provide documentation that proves your ineligibility.

Special Considerations for Teen Drivers

1. **Driver's Education and Training:**
   o **Driver's Education:** Teens must complete a state-approved driver's education course that includes at least 30 hours of classroom instruction.
   o **Driver's Training:** Additionally, teens must complete at least six hours of behind-the-wheel professional driver training.

2. **Provisional Licensing Requirements:**
   o **Learner's Permit:** Teens can apply for a learner's permit at 15½ years old after completing driver's education. They must practice driving with a licensed adult (25 years or older) and complete at least 50 hours of supervised driving, including 10 hours at night.
   o **Provisional License:** At 16 years old, after holding a learner's permit for at least six months and completing the required driving practice, teens can apply for a provisional driver's license. For the first 12 months, provisional license holders are restricted from driving between 11 p.m. and 5 a.m. and cannot transport passengers under 20 years old without a licensed adult present.

Additional Requirements for Minors:

- **Parental Consent:** Applicants under 18 need a parent or guardian to sign the application and accept financial responsibility. If parents share joint custody, both must sign.
- **Behind-the-Wheel Training Validation:** The instruction permit cannot be used until starting behind-the-wheel training with an instructor who will validate the permit.

Special Considerations for Senior Drivers

Senior drivers often have unique needs and concerns regarding driving, as it requires certain physical, visual, and mental abilities. While everyone aims to drive as long as possible, there may come a time when limiting or stopping driving becomes necessary. Here are important considerations and guidelines for senior drivers:

Renewal Process

Senior drivers must renew their licenses more frequently, usually every five years. If you are 70 years old or older when your driver's license expires, you are required to renew your driver's license in person, unless otherwise instructed by DMV. The renewal process includes knowledge and vision tests to ensure driving capabilities. If you do not pass these tests, you may be issued a temporary driver's license. DMV sends a renewal notice to your address of record about 60 days before your driver's license expires. If you do not receive a renewal notice, complete a Driver License or Identification Card Application at dmv.ca.gov/dlservices or at a DMV office.

Refresher Courses

Senior drivers are recommended to take refresher driving courses to stay updated on the latest road rules and safe driving practices. These courses can help improve driving skills and ensure safety on the road.

Medical Conditions

Seniors with medical conditions that could affect their driving abilities must provide medical documentation and may be subject to additional testing. It is crucial to monitor one's health and understand how it may impact driving skills.

Warning Signs of Unsafe Driving

It is important to recognize the warning signs of unsafe driving, which include:

- Getting lost in familiar places.
- Dents and scrapes on the car, fences, mailboxes, garage doors, etc.
- Frequent close calls or collisions.

Safety Tips for Senior Drivers

Senior drivers may consider the following to enhance safety and confidence on the road:

- Limit or avoid driving at night. If night driving is necessary, choose well-lit routes.
- Drive during times when traffic is light.
- Avoid difficult intersections and opt for simpler routes.
- Drive short distances or limit driving to essential places.
- Avoid freeway driving.
- Install an additional right-side mirror to improve visibility.

Driver Skills Self-Assessment

To assess your driving skills, you can get the Driver Skills Self-Assessment Questionnaire by visiting dmv.ca.gov/driver-skills. This tool helps evaluate your current driving abilities and determine if any adjustments or improvements are needed.

By following these guidelines, senior drivers can maintain their independence and safety on the road while recognizing and addressing any limitations that may arise. For more information and sample tests, visit dmv.ca.gov/driver-ed.

Special Considerations for Non-English Speakers

1. **Language Assistance:** The California DMV offers written tests in multiple languages, and you can bring an interpreter for the behind-the-wheel test if needed. Interpreters may assist during the pre-drive inspection but cannot accompany you during the actual drive test. Only the examiner is allowed in the vehicle during the test, with exceptions made for training, service animals, and certain law enforcement situations. Recording devices are prohibited during the test. If a device cannot be turned off or disabled, it must be blocked to prevent visual or audio recording.

2. **Study Materials:** The California Driver Handbook and other study resources are available in several languages to aid in preparation for the written test.

By meeting these eligibility requirements and understanding the specific considerations for different types of drivers, you can ensure a smooth application process for your California driver's license.

Chapter II: Preparing for the Written Knowledge Test

Key Topics Covered in the Written Test

Traffic Laws and Regulations: This topic covers the rules of the road, including speed limits, freeway regulations, carpool lane rules, and laws regarding alcohol and drug use while driving. Mastery of these laws is crucial not only for passing the DMV test but also for ensuring safety on the road.

Right-of-Way Principles and Parking Regulations: Understanding who has the right-of-way in different driving scenarios is critical. This includes intersections, pedestrian crossings, and merging lanes. Additionally, this section tests your knowledge of where you can and cannot park, including understanding curb colors, no-parking zones, and the rules for parking in various environments such as hills and business districts. These principles help prevent accidents and ensure smooth traffic flow.

Road Signs, Traffic Signals, and Pavement Markings: Recognizing and understanding the meanings of various road signs is vital. This includes warning signs, informational signs, regulatory signs, and pedestrian signals. Knowing these signs helps you navigate the roads safely and legally. You'll also need to understand the significance of different traffic signals and pavement markings, including how to respond to them correctly.

Safe Driving Practices and Handling Hazards: This section covers defensive driving techniques, what to do in emergencies, safe driving speeds for different conditions, and how to share the road with other vehicles and pedestrians. You will also learn how to handle skids, hydroplaning, sun glare, and driving in various conditions such as rain, fog, snow, and high winds. Additionally, it includes how to minimize distractions and use technology safely while driving, as well as understanding the dangers of carbon monoxide poisoning and how to prevent it. This ensures that you are prepared for a variety of driving situations and can maintain focus to prevent accidents.

Study Tips and Techniques

Creating a Study Schedule: Dedicate specific times of the week for studying the driver handbook and taking practice tests. Consistency is key in retaining information.

Active vs. Passive Studying: Active studying involves more engagement with the material, such as taking notes, making flashcards, and teaching the content to another person. Passive studying involves reading or listening to the information without interacting with it. Combining both methods can be very effective.

Practice Test Strategies: When taking practice tests, treat them as if they are the actual exam. This will help you get used to the format and time constraints. Review your answers, especially the incorrect ones, to ensure you understand why you made mistakes.

Study Groups: Joining a study group can be beneficial. Discussing topics with others can improve your understanding and retention of the material. It also adds a social element to studying, which can make it more enjoyable and motivating.

Managing Test Stress and Anxiety

Test anxiety is a prevalent issue among students, characterized by intense stress and fear before or during exams. This anxiety can negatively impact performance by depleting working memory and causing a phenomenon known as "choking." By understanding the nature of test anxiety and learning how to manage it, students can significantly enhance both their academic performance and overall well-being.

The Nature of Test Anxiety

The high-pressure environment of exams often drives test anxiety. It's important to recognize that a certain amount of stress can be beneficial. Stress heightens our senses, increases focus, and can lead to better performance. However, excessive stress can lead to burnout and poor results. Thus, the goal is to manage stress to an optimal level where it enhances rather than hinders performance.

Three Main Fears of Exams

Test anxiety can often be traced back to three primary fears: the fear of the unknown, the fear of inadequacy, and the fear of the stakes. Each of these fears can be addressed with specific strategies to reduce their impact.

Fear of the Unknown

The fear of the unknown arises from uncertainty about the exam content, format, and environment. Reducing this fear involves making the exam as familiar as possible. One effective strategy is to recreate test conditions as closely as possible during study sessions. This could involve studying in the actual test location or a similar environment and simulating exam conditions, including timing and types of questions.

Another way to mitigate the fear of the unknown is to seek information from your professor. Many students assume that if the professor didn't readily provide information in class, they won't give it out if asked. However, professors are often willing to clarify aspects of the exam if approached. Asking about the test format, types of questions, allowed materials, and duration can provide valuable insights.

Additionally, looking for old tests can help make the exam more predictable. Many student organizations maintain test banks, and websites like koofers.com offer databases of past exams. Accessing these resources can help students understand the test pattern and feel more prepared.

Fear of Inadequacy

The fear of inadequacy stems from the belief that one is not sufficiently prepared for the exam. Overcoming this fear requires thorough preparation and strategic revision. Consistent study throughout the semester is key. Using discipline hacks and planning techniques can help maintain a steady study schedule, reducing the need for last-minute cramming.

Identifying knowledge gaps is another crucial step. Reviewing notes and pinpointing areas where understanding is weak allows for focused revision. Creating a detailed study schedule for the weeks leading up to the exam can also be beneficial. This schedule should include all obligations, study sessions, and necessary breaks to maintain balance.

Active study techniques, such as making quizzes and engaging in active recall, can enhance understanding and retention of the material. Boosting confidence through positive self-talk and acting confident can also help. Writing down worries before the test can clear the mind and allow for better focus during the exam.

Fear of the Stakes

The fear of the stakes is the belief that the outcome of the test will determine future success or failure. While it's natural to feel pressure, it's important to keep things in perspective. Understanding that one test does not define your future is crucial. Academic performance is only one aspect of overall success, along with value creation and relationship building.

Embracing the pressure and using it to sharpen focus can transform it into a positive force. Viewing the test as an opportunity to showcase knowledge rather than a life-defining moment can reduce anxiety. Recognizing that academic performance is a continuous journey and one test is just a part of it can also help manage this fear.

Additional Concerns: Perfectionism and Past Failures

Perfectionism can lead to unnecessary stress and unrealistic expectations. While striving for excellence is good, aiming for perfection can be detrimental. Setting realistic goals and accepting that mistakes are part of the learning process can alleviate this pressure.

Past failures can create a negative bias, making it easy to fear that history will repeat itself. It's essential to break this cycle and focus on the present. Analyzing past performances to understand what went wrong and changing study methods and preparation strategies can lead to better results.

Conclusion: Building a Resilient Mindset

Managing test anxiety is about building resilience and adopting effective strategies to tackle the underlying fears. By understanding and addressing the fear of the unknown, the fear of inadequacy, and the fear of the stakes, students can transform stress into a positive force that enhances performance. Preparation, perspective, and confidence are the best tools in overcoming test anxiety.

Adopting these strategies, practicing regularly, and maintaining a balanced approach to studies can make managing test stress and anxiety second nature. This, in turn, leads to better academic performance and a healthier, more positive outlook on exams.

Chapter III: Traffic Laws and Roadway Regulations

Traffic Laws and Rules of the Road

Understanding traffic laws and the rules of the road is foundational for passing the California DMV written test and for safe driving. This section will provide a comprehensive look at key regulations, driving guidelines, and legal requirements every driver in California should know.

Right-of-Way Principles: Determining Priority on the Road

Right-of-way rules are critical for delineating which party has priority in different traffic situations, thereby minimizing confusion and preventing collisions. It is important to not always assume others will yield the right-of-way to you. In some cases, relinquishing your right-of-way is necessary to avoid accidents.

Roundabouts

Traffic in a roundabout moves one-way around a central island. To navigate a roundabout safely:

1. Slow down as you approach.
2. Yield to all traffic in the roundabout.
3. Enter to the right when there is a sufficient gap.
4. Follow signs and lane markings.
5. Travel counter-clockwise without stopping or passing.
6. Signal when changing lanes or exiting.
7. If you miss your exit, continue around until you reach it again.

Choose your entry or exit lane based on your intended direction:

- **Right Turn**: Use the right lane and exit from it.
- **Straight**: Use any lane and exit from the same lane you entered.
- **Left Turn**: Enter and continue until you reach the desired exit.

Intersections

An intersection is where two roads converge. Controlled intersections have signs or traffic lights, while uncontrolled and blind intersections do not. Before entering an intersection, check left, right, and ahead for vehicles, bicyclists, and pedestrians, and be ready to slow down or stop if necessary. Pedestrians always have the right-of-way. Specific rules for navigating intersections include:

- **Without Stop or Yield Signs**: The first vehicle at the intersection has the right-of-way. If you arrive simultaneously with another vehicle, pedestrian, or bicyclist, yield to the one on your right. At a four-way stop, the first to stop should proceed first.

- **T-intersections without Stop or Yield Signs**: Vehicles on the through road have the right-of-way.
- **Turning Right**: Check for pedestrians crossing the street and be aware of motorcycles and bicycles beside you.
- **Turning Left**: Yield to pedestrians and oncoming vehicles that are close enough to pose a danger.
- **Entering Traffic**: Proceed cautiously and yield to traffic already in the lanes. Do not block an intersection if there isn't enough space to clear it before the traffic signal changes to red.
- **Green Traffic Signal Light**: Proceed with caution, always giving pedestrians the right-of-way.

Crosswalks

Crosswalks, marked with white or yellow lines, are designated for pedestrian use. Pedestrians have the right-of-way, marked or not. Stop at the limit line before a crosswalk to let pedestrians cross. Be prepared to stop at crosswalks with flashing lights.

Pedestrians

Pedestrians, including those using roller skates, skateboards, or mobility aids, are vulnerable road users with the right-of-way. They must follow road rules. When a pedestrian is crossing, drivers must exercise caution, reduce speed, or stop to ensure safe passage. Additional guidelines include:

- Do not pass a vehicle stopped at a crosswalk.
- Yield if a pedestrian makes eye contact.
- Allow enough time for pedestrians to cross safely, especially the elderly, those with small children, or with disabilities.

Pedestrians Who Are Blind

Pedestrians using guide dogs or white canes have the right-of-way at all times. Extra caution is needed when turning or backing up, especially with quiet vehicles like hybrids or electrics. Guidelines include:

- Do not stop in the middle of a crosswalk.
- Do not honk at a blind person.
- When a blind person pulls in their cane and steps away from the intersection, you may proceed.

Mountain Roads

On steep, narrow roads where two vehicles cannot pass, the vehicle facing uphill has the right-of-way. The downhill vehicle should back up, as it has better control moving uphill.

Speed Limits and Zones

Understanding and adhering to speed limits is crucial for safe driving. Speed limits are established to regulate traffic flow and reduce the risk of accidents. This chapter provides an overview of different speed limits and zones, and the importance of following them.

General Speed Limits

Speed limits vary depending on the type of road and area. Here are the general speed limits you should be aware of:

- **Highways and Freeways:** The maximum speed limit on most California highways is 65 mph. Some highways may have speed limits up to 70 mph. Always look for and obey posted speed limits.
- **Two-Lane Undivided Highways:** The maximum speed limit on two-lane undivided highways is 55 mph unless otherwise posted.
- **Residential Areas:** The speed limit in residential areas is typically 25 mph unless otherwise posted.
- **Business Districts:** The speed limit in business districts is usually 25 mph unless otherwise posted.

Special Speed Limits

Certain areas have special speed limits to enhance safety for vulnerable road users and adapt to specific conditions:

- **School Zones:** When driving within 500 to 1,000 feet of a school while children are outside or crossing the street, the speed limit is 25 mph. Some school zones may have speed limits as low as 15 mph. Always be alert for children and school safety patrols.
- **Construction Zones:** Speed limits in construction zones are typically reduced to ensure the safety of road workers. Fines for speeding in these zones are often doubled. Look for and obey posted signs indicating reduced speed limits.
- **Blind Intersections:** At intersections where your view is obstructed by trees, buildings, or other objects, the speed limit is 15 mph.
- **Alleys:** The speed limit in alleys is 15 mph.
- **Railroad Crossings:** The speed limit is 15 mph within 100 feet of a railroad crossing where you cannot see the tracks for 400 feet in both directions. You may drive faster if the crossing is controlled by gates, a warning signal, or a flagman.

Speed Limit Adjustments

Adjusting your speed according to road, traffic, and weather conditions is essential for safe driving. Here are some situations where you should reduce your speed:

- **Heavy Traffic and Bad Weather:** In heavy traffic or adverse weather conditions (rain, fog, snow), reduce your speed to maintain control and increase stopping distance.
- **Curves and Intersections:** Slow down when approaching curves and intersections to ensure you can stop if necessary.
- **Pedestrian Areas:** Reduce speed in areas with high pedestrian activity, such as shopping districts, parks, and residential neighborhoods.

Minimum Speed Limits

Driving too slowly can also be dangerous. Minimum speed limits are enforced to ensure a smooth flow of traffic and prevent accidents:

- **Highways and Freeways:** While there is no universally set minimum speed limit, driving too slowly on highways and freeways can impede traffic and increase the risk of accidents. If you are driving significantly slower than the flow of traffic, use the rightmost lane.
- **Obstructing Traffic:** It is illegal to drive so slowly that you obstruct the normal flow of traffic. If you are causing a backup, pull over safely and allow other vehicles to pass.

Speed Limit Enforcement

Speed limits are enforced by law enforcement officers to maintain road safety. Here are some common methods of enforcement:

- **Speed Cameras:** Automated cameras are used in some areas to detect and ticket speeding vehicles.
- **Radar Guns:** Police officers use radar guns to measure vehicle speed and identify speeders.
- **Pacing:** An officer may follow a suspected speeder to determine their speed.

Consequences of Speeding

Exceeding the speed limit can have serious consequences:

- **Fines and Penalties:** Speeding tickets result in fines, which can be higher in construction and school zones. Accumulating too many tickets can lead to increased insurance rates and license suspension.
- **Accidents and Injuries:** Higher speeds increase the severity of accidents, leading to more significant injuries and fatalities.
- **Legal Consequences:** Extreme speeding can result in reckless driving charges, which carry severe penalties, including jail time.

Safe Speed Practices

To ensure you are driving at a safe speed:

- **Observe Speed Limits:** Always pay attention to posted speed limit signs and adjust your speed accordingly.
- **Stay Aware of Road Conditions:** Adapt your speed to match road, traffic, and weather conditions.
- **Use Common Sense:** Drive at a speed that is safe for the current conditions, even if it is below the posted speed limit.

By understanding and adhering to speed limits and zones, you contribute to the safety and efficiency of the roadways. Always drive responsibly and be mindful of the conditions around you.

Parking Regulations

Proper parking is essential for ensuring safety, accessibility, and the smooth flow of traffic. This chapter outlines various parking regulations to help you avoid fines, penalties, and potential hazards.

General Parking Rules

When parking your vehicle, always ensure it is positioned safely and legally. Park in designated areas, following signs and markings indicating where parking is allowed. Ensure your vehicle is fully within the designated space without encroaching on adjacent spaces or obstructing traffic. Avoid parking in a manner that blocks driveways, sidewalks, crosswalks, or intersections. Additionally, make sure your vehicle is visible to other drivers and pedestrians, especially at night, by using parking lights or hazard lights if necessary.

No Parking Zones

Parking is prohibited in several areas to maintain safety and accessibility. Do not park within 15 feet of a fire hydrant, in crosswalks, or on sidewalks. Avoid parking within 20 feet of intersections to ensure clear visibility for drivers. Never block driveways, park in bus stops, or load/unload zones unless you are a commercial vehicle performing such activities.

Time-Limited Parking

In some areas, parking is allowed only for a limited time to ensure turnover and availability. Look for signs indicating time restrictions, such as "2-hour parking," and ensure you move your vehicle before the time limit expires. For metered parking, pay attention to parking meters and keep them updated to avoid fines.

Residential Parking

Residential areas often have specific parking regulations to ensure residents have access to parking spaces. Some areas require permits for parking; ensure you have the appropriate permit displayed in your vehicle. Be aware of street sweeping schedules, which may prohibit parking on certain days and times to allow for street cleaning.

Disabled Parking

Disabled parking spaces are reserved for individuals with disabilities who have the appropriate permits. These spaces are typically located near building entrances for accessibility. Only park in disabled parking spaces if you have a valid disabled parking permit or license plate. Misuse of these permits can result in hefty fines and penalties.

Parking on Hills

When parking on hills, take additional precautions to prevent your vehicle from rolling. For uphill parking, turn your front wheels away from the curb and set the parking brake. For downhill parking, turn your front wheels towards the curb. If there is no curb, turn your wheels towards the shoulder of the road.

Emergency Parking

In emergencies, you may need to park your vehicle in a non-standard location. Ensure your vehicle is visible and does not obstruct traffic. Use hazard lights to alert other drivers to your presence. If possible, move your vehicle to a safe location as soon as the emergency is resolved.

Parallel Parking

Parallel parking involves parking your vehicle in line with the road and other parked vehicles. Here's how to parallel park:

1. Find a space at least three feet longer than your vehicle and signal your intention to park.
2. Pull up alongside the vehicle in front of the space, leaving about two feet between the vehicles. Stop when your rear bumper aligns with the front of your parking space.
3. Check your blind spots and ensure there are no approaching vehicles or pedestrians.
4. Begin backing into the space at a 45-degree angle.
5. Straighten your wheels when your rear wheel is within 18 inches of the curb, adjusting as needed to be parallel and within 18 inches of the curb.
6. Turn off your vehicle and set the parking brake. Look for passing vehicles, bicycles, and motorcycles before exiting your vehicle.

Straight Line Backing

To back up in a straight line:

1. Check traffic and your blind spots.
2. Signal before pulling up to the curb, then cancel the signal once completed.
3. Begin backing up, maintaining a straight line for three vehicle lengths while staying within three feet of the curb.
4. Back at a smooth, safe speed, adjusting the steering wheel as needed to keep the vehicle straight.

Parking on a Hill

When parking on a hill, ensure your vehicle is secure to prevent rolling due to equipment failure. Set the parking brake and leave the vehicle in park or in gear for manual transmission. If on a sloping driveway, turn the wheels to prevent rolling into the street. When headed downhill, turn your front wheels into the curb or towards the side of the road. When headed uphill, turn your front wheels away from the curb and let your vehicle roll back slightly until the wheel gently touches the curb. If there is no curb, turn the wheels so the vehicle will roll away from the center of the road if the brakes fail.

Parking at Colored Curbs

Colored curbs indicate specific parking rules:

- **White:** Stop only long enough to pick up or drop off passengers.
- **Green:** Park for a limited time, as indicated by posted signs or curb markings.
- **Yellow:** Load and unload passengers or freight. Do not stop longer than posted. Noncommercial vehicles usually need to stay with the vehicle.
- **Red:** No stopping, standing, or parking. Buses may stop at red zones marked for buses only.
- **Blue:** Parking for disabled persons or those driving a disabled person with a special placard or license plate. For more information on disabled parking placards and plates, visit dmv.ca.gov/disabled-person-parking.

Illegal Parking

Avoid parking or leaving your vehicle in the following areas:

- Where a "No Parking" sign is posted.
- On marked or unmarked crosswalks.
- On sidewalks or in front of driveways.
- Within three feet of a sidewalk ramp for disabled persons.
- In front of or on a curb that provides wheelchair access to a sidewalk.
- In the crosshatched area next to a designated disabled parking space.
- In spaces designated for parking or fueling zero-emission vehicles, unless driving such a vehicle.
- In a tunnel or on a bridge unless permitted by signs.

- Within 15 feet of a fire hydrant or fire station driveway.
- Between a safety zone and the curb.
- Double parked.
- On the wrong side of the street or on a freeway, except in emergencies, when required by law enforcement, or where specifically permitted.

If you must stop on a freeway, park completely off the pavement and stay in your vehicle with the doors locked until help arrives. A vehicle stopped, parked, or left standing on a freeway for more than four hours may be removed.

Essential Roadway Regulations and Guidelines

This chapter covers various critical roadway regulations and guidelines to ensure your safety and adherence to the law.

Evading Law Enforcement

Using a motor vehicle to evade law enforcement is a misdemeanor punishable by up to one year in county jail. Causing serious injury while evading law enforcement can result in up to seven years in state prison. Manslaughter during such an evasion can lead to four to ten years in state prison. If an unlicensed person is caught driving your vehicle, it may be impounded for 30 days.

Speed Contests and Reckless Driving

Engaging in reckless driving or speed contests that cause injury to another person can result in imprisonment, fines, or both.

Points on Your Driver's Record

The DMV monitors your driving record. If cited for a traffic violation, you must sign the ticket as a promise to appear in court. Failure to appear (FTA) can result in a suspended license. Traffic convictions and collisions remain on your record for at least 36 months. Your license may be suspended if your record shows:

- 4 points in 12 months
- 6 points in 24 months
- 8 points in 36 months

Traffic Violator School

For a one-point traffic violation, you might be allowed to attend traffic violator school to keep the citation off your insurance record, although it remains on your driving record. This option is available once every 18 months. Completion is reported to the court, and you receive a completion receipt.

Suspension or Revocation

Accumulating too many points can result in being labeled a negligent driver, leading to probation, suspension, or revocation of your driving privilege. You have the right to a hearing in these cases. The DMV will notify you of any action taken and inform you of your rights.

Maintaining Your Minor's (Provisional) Driver's License

If you are a minor with traffic violations or collisions within the first 12 months of obtaining your license, the DMV may restrict or suspend your driving privilege:

- One at-fault collision or traffic violation: No immediate action, but a warning.
- Two at-fault collisions, two traffic violations, or one of each: You cannot drive for 30 days unless accompanied by a licensed adult aged 25 or older.
- Three at-fault collisions, three traffic violations, or a combination: Your driving privilege will be suspended for six months, and you will be on probation for one year. Further violations during probation will result in additional suspensions.

If convicted of using alcohol or controlled substances, the court will order the DMV to suspend your license for one year or delay your eligibility to apply for a license. Turning 18 does not remove existing restrictions, suspensions, or probation sentences.

Administrative Hearing

You have the right to request an administrative hearing within 10 days of being served notice or 14 days from the notice date. This hearing allows you to present evidence and witnesses, testify, and cross-examine witnesses. You can be represented by an attorney at your expense. For more information, visit the DMV website.

Unsafe Driver

If you know someone who can no longer drive safely, you can submit a Request for Driver Reexamination to the DMV. Forms are available on the DMV website.

Record Confidentiality

Most information in your driver's record is public, except for physical or mental conditions, address, and social security number. You can request a copy of your driver's record online or at a DMV kiosk. For more information, visit the DMV website.

By understanding and following these regulations, you contribute to safer roads for everyone.

Prohibited Actions:

- **Smoking with a Minor in the Vehicle:** Smoking in a vehicle with a minor present is illegal and can result in fines.
- **Abandoning Animals on a Highway:** Abandoning animals on a highway is punishable by a fine of up to $1,000, six months in jail, or both.
- **Overloaded Vehicles:** Do not drive a vehicle that is so overloaded that it affects your control or visibility.
- **Unsecured Loads:** Ensure all loads on your vehicle are secure and do not pose a safety hazard.
- **Extended Cargo:** Do not transport anything on a passenger vehicle that extends beyond the fenders on the left side or more than 6 inches beyond the fenders on the right side. If cargo extends more than 4 feet from the rear bumper, it must be marked with a 12-inch red or fluorescent orange square flag during the day and two red lights at night.
- **Passengers in Truck Beds:** Do not allow passengers to ride in the back of a pickup or other truck unless it has secure seats and seat belts.
- **Transporting Animals:** Animals in the back of a pickup or other truck must be properly secured to prevent them from falling, jumping, or being thrown from the vehicle.
- **Video Monitors:** Vehicles should not be equipped with video monitors visible to the driver unless they display vehicle information, navigation, media, or radio.
- **Throwing Flaming Objects:** It is illegal to throw cigarettes, cigars, or other flaming substances from your vehicle.
- **Obstructing Windows:** Do not place signs or objects on the front windshield or side/rear windows that block your view. Objects can only be affixed in the following locations:
  o A 7-inch square on the lower corner of the passenger's side windshield or the lower corner of the rear window.
  o A 5-inch square on the lower corner of the driver's side window.
  o A 5-inch square in the center uppermost portion of the windshield for an electronic toll payment device.
  o On the side windows behind the driver.
- **Funeral Processions:** Do not interfere with a funeral procession. Funeral processions have the right-of-way and are led by a traffic officer. Vehicles in the procession will have windshield markers and headlights on.
- **License Plates:** Do not drive with an illegible or altered license plate.

Chapter IV: Understanding Traffic Signals and Road Signs

In this chapter, I will explain in detail the various traffic signs that you will encounter on the road. Understanding these signs is crucial for safe and efficient driving. To complement this chapter, I have included a link that will lead you to a page with color pictures of the signs, allowing you to visually familiarize yourself with them. By reviewing both the descriptions and the images, you will gain a comprehensive understanding of traffic signs and their meanings.

Scan the QR code to access the full-color digital versions of this book, allowing you to view all road signs in their true colors:

Pedestrian Signals

WALK or Walking Person: Indicates it is safe to cross the street. Pedestrians should proceed, checking for any turning vehicles.

DON'T WALK or Raised Hand: Signals that crossing is not allowed. Pedestrians should not enter the crosswalk.

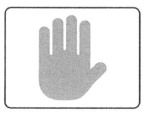

Pedestrian Push Button: When pressed, this button activates the WALK signal, often used at intersections where pedestrian signals only change when activated.

No Pedestrian Signals: If no specific pedestrian signals are present, pedestrians should follow the vehicle traffic lights for guidance on when to cross safely.

Flashing DON'T WALK or Flashing Raised Hand: Warns that the light is about to change, and it is too late to begin crossing safely. Pedestrians already in the crosswalk should complete their crossing. Drivers must continue to yield to pedestrians.

Diagonal Crossing: Allows pedestrians to cross in any direction at the same time while all traffic signals for vehicles are red. This should only be done when the WALK signal is displayed.

Numbers: Shows a countdown of the seconds remaining for pedestrians to complete the crossing, helping manage crossing time effectively.

Sounds: Beeping, chirping, or verbal messages provide auditory guidance for blind or visually impaired pedestrians, indicating when it is safe to cross.

Traffic Signals

Solid Green Light: Indicates it's safe to go. Yield to any vehicles, bicyclists, or pedestrians still in the intersection. Do not enter the intersection unless you are sure you can clear it without stopping.

Green Arrow: Provides the right to make a protected turn in the direction of the arrow while opposing traffic is stopped.

Solid Yellow Light: Signals CAUTION, indicating the light will soon turn red. You should stop if it is safe to do so; otherwise, proceed with caution.

Yellow Arrow: Signifies the end of a protected turn period. Prepare to stop unless already in the intersection or unable to stop safely.

Flashing Yellow Light: Proceed through the intersection with caution. There is no need to stop but remain alert.

Flashing Yellow Arrow: Allows you to turn left but without the right of way. Yield to oncoming traffic and pedestrians, turning only when safe.

Solid Red Light: Means STOP. Turning right on a red light is permitted unless a sign explicitly prohibits it. Ensure you come to a complete stop, yield to pedestrians and other traffic, and only proceed when safe.

Red Arrow: Indicates a full stop and no turning in the direction of the arrow. Wait until the signal changes to a green light or green arrow.

Flashing Red Light: Equivalent to a stop sign. After stopping, proceed when it's safe, yielding to all other traffic and pedestrians.

Traffic Light Not Working: Treat the intersection as a four-way stop sign. Proceed only when it's your turn and safe to do so.

Road Signs
Lane Usage and Turns Road Signs

STOP Sign: This sign requires drivers to make a complete stop at the crosswalk or limit line before proceeding. If there is no crosswalk or limit line, stop before entering the intersection, ensuring it's safe to proceed.

Red YIELD Sign: When encountering this sign, drivers must slow down and be prepared to stop, yielding to all traffic, bicyclists, or pedestrians before continuing.

Red and White Regulatory Sign: This type of sign provides specific instructions such as "DO NOT ENTER," guiding drivers to avoid entering restricted areas or roads, which helps control traffic flow and enhances safety.

WRONG WAY Sign: This sign alerts drivers that they are going the wrong direction on a roadway. If you see this sign, safely reverse your direction when possible. At night, if road reflectors shine red in your headlights, it indicates you are driving the wrong way.

Red Circle with a Red Line Through It: This prohibition sign shows a specific action that is not allowed, such as no smoking or no U-turns, ensuring drivers avoid these prohibited actions to maintain safety and compliance with local laws.

Yellow and Black Circular Sign or X-shaped Sign: These signs warn drivers that they are approaching a railroad crossing. Drivers should look and listen for trains and be prepared to stop if necessary.

RR Railroad Crossing Sign: Accompanying railroad crossings, this sign provides additional instructions for how to act in emergencies or if a vehicle stalls on the tracks, enhancing safety at these crossings.

5-sided Sign (School Zone Sign): Located in school zones, this sign advises drivers to slow down and be prepared to stop for children crossing the street, increasing safety in areas where young pedestrians are present.

Diamond-shaped Sign: These signs alert drivers to special road conditions or potential dangers ahead, prompting them to adjust their driving accordingly.

White Rectangular Sign: These signs communicate important rules like speed limits and driving directions, ensuring drivers follow legal and safe practices on the roads.

Warning Signs: These signs caution drivers about potential hazards or changes in driving conditions that may involve pedestrians, bicyclists, schools, and playgrounds, urging drivers to proceed with increased caution.

Highway Construction And Maintenance Signs are crucial for alerting drivers to changes or potential hazards in their driving environment due to roadwork

Hazardous Loads Placards are used to indicate vehicles carrying dangerous or hazardous materials. These placards are diamond-shaped and display specific symbols and colors that correspond to the type of hazard involved, such as flammable, toxic, or corrosive substances.

Road Closed Signs

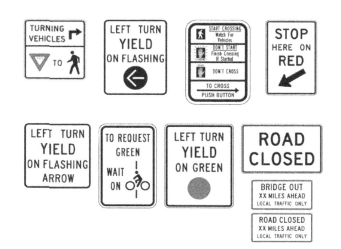

Warning Signs: These signs caution drivers about potential hazards or changes in driving conditions that may involve pedestrians, bicyclists, schools, and playgrounds, urging drivers to proceed with increased caution.

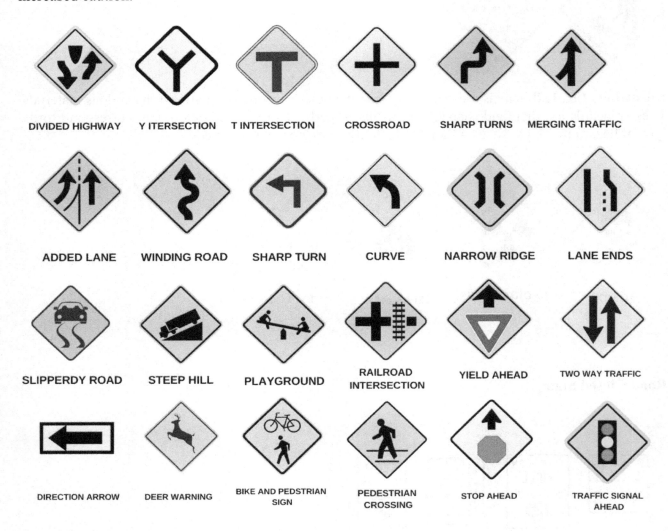

DIVIDED HIGHWAY	Y ITERSECTION	T INTERSECTION	CROSSROAD	SHARP TURNS	MERGING TRAFFIC
ADDED LANE	WINDING ROAD	SHARP TURN	CURVE	NARROW RIDGE	LANE ENDS
SLIPPERDY ROAD	STEEP HILL	PLAYGROUND	RAILROAD INTERSECTION	YIELD AHEAD	TWO WAY TRAFFIC
DIRECTION ARROW	DEER WARNING	BIKE AND PEDSTRIAN SIGN	PEDESTRIAN CROSSING	STOP AHEAD	TRAFFIC SIGNAL AHEAD

Pavement Markings

Pavement markings are critical for guiding and regulating traffic flow on the roads. They provide important information to drivers about lane usage, passing, stopping, and pedestrian crossings. This chapter details the different types of pavement markings and their meanings to help you navigate the roads safely and legally.

Lane Markings

Lane markings on road surfaces help drivers know which part of the road to use and understand traffic

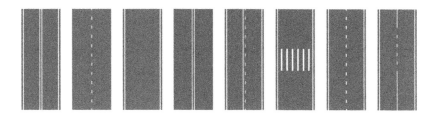

rules.

A **single solid yellow line** marks the center of a road with two-way traffic. Do not pass a vehicle in front of you if there is only one lane of traffic going your direction and a solid yellow line on your side of the road.

Double solid yellow lines indicate that passing is not allowed. Stay to the right of these lines unless you are in a high-occupancy vehicle (HOV) carpool lane with a designated entrance on the left, instructed by construction or other signs to drive on the other side of the road because your side is closed or blocked, or turning left across a single set of double yellow lines to enter or exit a driveway or private road or make a U-turn. Two sets of solid double yellow lines spaced two or more feet apart are considered a barrier. Do not drive on or over this barrier, make a left turn, or make a U-turn across it, except at designated openings.

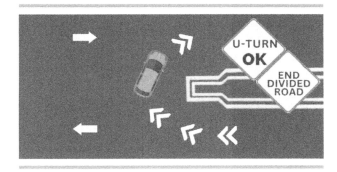

A **broken yellow line** indicates you may pass if the broken line is next to your driving lane. Only pass when it is safe.

A **single solid white line** marks traffic lanes going in the same direction, including one-way streets.

Double solid white lines indicate a lane barrier between a regular use and a preferential use lane, such as a carpool (HOV) lane. You may also see double solid white lines in or near freeway on and off ramps. Never change lanes over double solid white lines. Wait until you see a single broken white line.

Broken white lines separate traffic lanes on roads with two or more lanes in the same direction.

Ending freeway and street lanes are usually marked with large broken lines. If you are driving in a lane marked with broken lines, be prepared to exit the freeway or for the lane to end. Look for a sign that tells you to exit or merge.

A **yield line** is a solid white line of triangles that shows approaching vehicles where to yield or stop. The triangles point towards approaching vehicles

Center Left Turn Lanes

A **center left turn lane** is located in the middle of a two-way street and is marked on both sides by two painted lines: the inner line is broken, and the outer line is solid. Use the center left turn lane to prepare for and make a left turn or U-turn. It is not a regular traffic lane or passing lane. You may only drive for 200 feet in the center left turn lane. To turn left from this lane, signal, check your blind spots, and merge completely into the center left turn lane so you do not block traffic. Turn when it is safe.

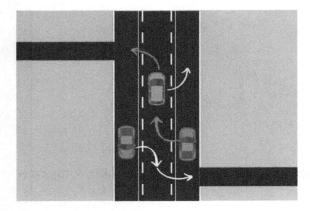

Crosswalks and Stop Lines

Crosswalks are marked with white lines, either solid or in a ladder pattern, indicating pedestrian crossing areas. Drivers must yield to pedestrians in crosswalks. Not all crosswalks are marked, so be cautious at intersections.

Stop lines are wide white lines painted across a traffic lane, indicating where vehicles must stop at intersections or traffic signals. Stop your vehicle before the stop line.

Special Markings

School zones are marked with yellow paint and school symbols, indicating areas where children are likely to cross the street. Reduce your speed and be prepared to stop.

Bike lanes are for bicyclists only and run alongside vehicle traffic. They are typically marked by a single solid white line and signs and are sometimes painted bright green to make them easier to see. It is illegal to drive in a bicycle lane unless you are parking (where permitted), entering or leaving the road, or turning (within 200 feet of an intersection).

HOV lanes (High Occupancy Vehicle) are special lanes reserved for carpools, buses, motorcycles, or low-emission vehicles with decals. The road surface in an HOV lane is marked with a diamond symbol and the words Carpool Lane. Do not cross over double solid lines to enter or exit an HOV lane. Use designated entrances and exits.

Arrows indicate the direction of travel in lanes. Turn arrows indicate where you must turn, while straight arrows indicate where you must go straight. Follow the direction indicated by the arrows.

Bike lanes are for bicyclists only and run alongside vehicle traffic. They are typically marked by a single solid white line and signs and are sometimes painted bright green to make them easier to see. It is illegal to drive in a bicycle lane unless you are parking (where permitted), entering or leaving the road, or turning (within 200 feet of

Curb Markings

- **Green curb**: Allows for limited-time parking, as specified by signs or curb markings.
- **White curb**: Indicates areas where you can stop only long enough to pick up or drop off passengers.
- **Yellow curb**: Used for loading and unloading passengers or freight. Noncommercial vehicles are usually required to stay with the vehicle.
- **Blue curb**: Reserved for disabled persons with a special placard or license plate.
- **Red curb**: Indicates no stopping, standing, or parking.

Passing lanes

Passing lanes are designated lanes on a multi-lane road, typically the far-left lane, used specifically for overtaking slower vehicles safely.

Painted Messages

Yield lines are rows of small triangles extending across the lane, indicating where you should yield to oncoming traffic or pedestrians. These are often found at roundabouts and mid-block crosswalks.

Sharrows (Shared Lane Markings) consist of a bike symbol with two chevrons above it, indicating that the lane is shared between bicyclists and motorists. Motorists should be prepared to share the lane with cyclists.

Reflective Markings

Reflective markers enhance the visibility of lane markings, especially at night and in poor weather conditions. They can be different colors, with each color indicating a different type of marking:

- **White reflectors**: Used to mark lane lines or the right edge of the roadway.
- **Yellow reflectors**: Mark the left edge of the roadway on divided highways and one-way streets.
- **Red reflectors**: Indicate areas not to be entered or used, such as the wrong side of a divided highway.

By understanding and following pavement markings, you can navigate roads more safely and efficiently.

Chapter V: Driving Basics and Maneuvering

Driving Basics

Mastering the fundamentals of driving is essential for the safe and confident operation of a vehicle. This chapter covers the essential driving skills and knowledge required to navigate the road safely.

Starting Your Vehicle

1. **Adjust Your Seat and Mirrors:**
   o Ensure you are seated comfortably with a clear view of the road.
   o Adjust the rearview and side mirrors to minimize blind spots.
2. **Fasten Your Seat Belt:**
   o Always wear your seat belt and ensure all passengers do the same.
3. **Check Your Surroundings:**
   o Before starting the engine, check your surroundings for any obstacles, pedestrians, or other vehicles.
4. **Start the Engine:**
   o Insert the key into the ignition or press the start button. Ensure the vehicle is in park (P) or neutral (N).

Moving Your Vehicle

1. **Foot on the Brake:**
   o Keep your foot on the brake pedal when shifting gears.
2. **Shift into Gear:**
   o Shift the gear lever to drive (D) for automatic transmissions or first gear for manual transmissions.
3. **Release the Parking Brake:**
   o Ensure the parking brake is fully released before moving.
4. **Check for Traffic:**
   o Look over your shoulder and check mirrors for oncoming traffic before merging into the lane.
5. **Accelerate Smoothly:**
   o Gently press the accelerator to move forward, maintaining a smooth and steady speed.

Steering and Control

1. **Hand Position:**
   o Place your hands at the 9 and 3 o'clock positions on the steering wheel for optimal control.

2. **Hand-to-Hand Steering (Push/Pull):**
   - Keep your hands on the wheel, pushing and pulling without crossing them over.
3. **Hand-Over-Hand Steering:**
   - Use this method for low-speed maneuvers, such as parking or recovering from a skid.
4. **One-Hand Steering:**
   - Only use one-hand steering when turning while backing up or when operating vehicle controls.
5. **Maintaining Lane Position:**
   - Stay centered in your lane and avoid drifting. Use lane markings as a guide.

Braking and Stopping

1. **Foot on the Brake:**
   - Gently press the brake pedal to slow down or stop the vehicle.
2. **Smooth Braking:**
   - Apply consistent pressure to the brake pedal to avoid sudden stops and jerks.
3. **Stopping Distance:**
   - Maintain a safe distance from the vehicle ahead to allow adequate stopping time.
4. **Using the Parking Brake:**
   - Engage the parking brake when parking the vehicle to prevent rolling.

Turning and Lane Changes

1. **Signal Your Intentions:**
   - Use your turn signals to indicate your intention to turn or change lanes.
2. **Check Blind Spots:**
   - Look over your shoulder to check blind spots before turning or changing lanes.
3. **Smooth Turns:**
   - Slow down before turning and accelerate gently as you complete the turn.
4. **Lane Changes:**
   - Signal, check mirrors and blind spots, and smoothly merge into the desired lane.

Signals, Horns, and Headlights

1. **Signaling:**
   - Always signal when you turn, change lanes, slow down, or stop. Signal at least 100 feet before your action, and remember to turn off your signal once the maneuver is completed.
2. **Using Your Horn:**
   - Use your horn to alert other drivers of your presence or to warn them of a hazard.
3. **Using Your Headlights:**
   - Your headlights help you see what is in front of you and make it easier for other drivers to see your vehicle. Use your headlights:

- When it is too dark to see from 1,000 feet away.
- From 30 minutes after sunset until 30 minutes before sunrise.
- In adverse weather conditions like fog, rain, or snow.
- On mountain roads and in tunnels.
- When a road sign indicates headlights are required.
- To help other drivers see your vehicle, especially when the sun is low on the horizon.

4. **Using Your Emergency Flashers:**
   - If you see a collision or hazard ahead, warn drivers behind you by turning on your emergency flashers, lightly tapping your brake pedal three or four times, or using hand signals when slowing and stopping.

Health and Driving

1. **Vision:**
   - Ensure you can see hazards, judge distances, adjust to traffic speeds, and read road signs.
2. **Hearing:**
   - Be able to hear horns, sirens, and other sounds that may alert you to potential hazards. Note that it is illegal to wear a headset or earplugs in both ears while driving.
3. **Fatigue and Drowsiness:**
   - Avoid driving when tired, as it can impair your vision and increase reaction time to hazards.
4. **Physical and Mental Alertness:**
   - Stay alert to quickly decide the correct course of action in any traffic situation, including unexpected ones.
5. **Medications:**
   - Be aware that prescription and over-the-counter medications can affect your ability to drive safely. Always read medication labels and know their effects.

Turns

Turning is a fundamental aspect of driving that requires attention to safety and road regulations. This chapter provides a detailed guide on how to execute various types of turns safely and legally.

Hand Signals for Driving

When your vehicle's signal lights are not functioning or are not visible, using hand signals is a crucial way to communicate your intentions to other drivers. Here's a brief explanation of how to signal with your hands:

Left Turn: Extend your left arm straight out horizontally from the driver's window.

Right Turn: Extend your left arm out and upward, forming a right angle at the elbow.

Stop or Slow Down: Extend your left arm out and downward, forming an angle at the elbow with the palm facing backward.

Using these hand signals correctly ensures that you can communicate effectively with other road users, promoting safety and preventing misunderstandings on the road.

Right Turns

1. **Preparation:**
   - Drive close to the right edge of the road. If there is a designated right-turn lane, enter it when the lane opens.
   - You may drive in a bike lane no more than 200 feet before the turn, but always check for bicyclists in your blind spots.
2. **Signaling:**
   - Signal about 100 feet before making the turn.
3. **Executing the Turn:**
   - Look over your right shoulder and reduce your speed.
   - Stop behind the limit line (a wide white line indicating where vehicles should stop before an intersection or crosswalk). If there is no limit line, stop before entering the crosswalk. If no crosswalk is present, stop before the intersection.
   - Look both ways (left-right-left) and proceed with the turn when it is safe, completing your turn in the right lane without swinging wide.
4. **Right Turn on Red:**
   - You may turn right on a red light after a complete stop unless a sign indicates otherwise. Follow the same steps as a regular right turn.
5. **Right Turn on Red Arrow:**
   - It is illegal to turn right if you are stopped at a red arrow light. Wait for the green light.
6. **Public Transit Bus Lane:**
   - Do not drive, stop, or park in a bus-only lane except to cross it to make a right turn.
7. **Right Turn into a Dedicated Lane:**
   - If the road has a dedicated right-turn lane that does not merge into another lane, you can make your turn without stopping, even on a red light. However, always yield to pedestrians.

Left Turns

1. **Preparation:**
   - Drive close to the center divider or into the left-turn lane.
   - Enter a designated left-turn lane at its opening. Do not cross solid lines.
2. **Signaling:**

- o Signal about 100 feet before the turn.
3. **Executing the Turn:**
   - o Look over your left shoulder and reduce your speed.
   - o Stop behind the limit line or before entering the crosswalk or intersection if no limit line is present.
   - o Look both ways (left-right-left) and start your turn when it is safe.
   - o Complete your turn in the left lane closest to the center divider. Do not turn the steering wheel prematurely, as this could push you into oncoming traffic if hit from behind.
4. **Left Turn on Red:**
   - o You may turn left on a red light when turning from a one-way street onto another one-way street unless prohibited by a sign. Yield to other traffic and pedestrians.

Right Turn onto a Road with a Dedicated Lane

This lane allows vehicles to turn right without merging into other lanes of traffic, ensuring a smooth and safe turn. Typically, these lanes are marked with signs and road markings indicating their purpose. When approaching such a lane, drivers can make the turn without stopping, even if the traffic light is red, as long as they yield to pedestrians and other vehicles that have the right-of-way.

U-Turns

1. **Legal U-Turns:**
   - o Across a double yellow line when safe.
   - o In residential areas if no vehicles are approaching within 200 feet.
   - o At intersections on a green light or arrow unless prohibited.
   - o On divided highways where an opening is provided.
2. **Illegal U-Turns:**
   - o Where prohibited by a sign.

- o At or on a railroad crossing.
- o On a divided highway crossing a curb or set of double yellow lines.
- o Where visibility is limited to less than 200 feet in each direction.
- o On one-way streets.
- o In front of fire stations or in business districts.

- **Left Turn from a Two-Way Street:**

  - Begin in the left lane closest to the middle of the street. End the turn in the same lane on the new road.

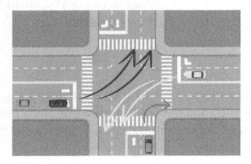

- **Left Turn from a One-Way Street to Another One-Way Street:**

  - Start from the far-left lane and complete the turn in any open lane.

- **Left Turn from a Two-Way Street to a One-Way Street:**

  - Start from the lane closest to the center of the street and end in any open lane on the one-way street.

- **Left Turn from a One-Way Street to a Two-Way Street:**

  - Begin in the far-left lane and end in the left lane closest to the center of the two-way street.

- **Turn at a "T" Intersection:**

  - Vehicles on the through road have the right-of-way. You may turn left or right from the center lane.

Braking

Proper braking techniques are essential for safe driving. Here are some guidelines to ensure you stop your vehicle safely:

1. **Gradual Braking:**
   - Remove your foot from the gas pedal to allow the vehicle to slow down naturally.
   - Lightly press the brake pedal until you come to a complete stop.
   - Maintain a safe distance from the vehicle in front of you, giving yourself ample time to brake smoothly.
2. **Stopping at a Limit Line:**
   - Do not cross over the limit line when stopping at an intersection.
   - Leave enough space between your vehicle and the one in front to see its rear wheels on the pavement.

Merging and Exiting

Merging onto Highways:

Highway traffic has the right-of-way. Follow these steps to merge safely:

- Position your vehicle in the proper lane on the on-ramp.
- Adjust your speed to match the flow of traffic.
- Merge into the highway when it is safe, ensuring there is enough space for your vehicle.
- Use mirrors and turn signals and look over your shoulder to check blind spots.
- Maintain a three-second following distance to ensure safe stopping space.

Exiting Highways:

Prepare for your exit by knowing the location and approaching it in the correct lane.

- Signal and check blind spots when changing lanes.
- Signal at least five seconds before you exit.
- Adjust your speed to exit safely, avoiding solid lines when exiting.

Crossing or Entering Traffic

When entering traffic from a full stop, ensure there is enough space to accelerate to the speed of traffic. For merging, entering, or exiting, a space of about half a block on city streets (150 feet) and a full block on highways (300 feet) is recommended. Even with a green light, do not cross an intersection if it is blocked by vehicles or pedestrians. When turning left, wait until oncoming vehicles start their turn before you begin yours.

Passing

Judging Space for Passing:

- Ensure there is enough space to pass without risking a collision.
- Consider oncoming vehicles, bicyclists, hills, curves, intersections, and road obstructions.
- Avoid passing within 100 feet of intersections, bridges, tunnels, railroad crossings, or other hazardous areas.

How to Pass:

- Signal your intention to pass.
- Check blind spots by looking over your shoulder.
- Move into the passing lane and accelerate to pass the vehicle.
- Signal again and return to your original lane safely.

Passing on the Right:

- You may pass on the right when:
    - The highway has two or more lanes going in your direction.
    - The driver ahead is turning left, and you can pass safely without driving off the paved road.

Being Passed:

- If another vehicle is passing you, maintain your lane position and speed, allowing them to pass safely.

Chapter VI: Safe Driving Practices

Defensive Driving Techniques

Safe driving practices are essential for ensuring the safety of everyone on the road, including drivers, passengers, pedestrians, and cyclists. This chapter outlines key strategies and habits for maintaining safety while driving.

Awareness and Scanning

Being aware of your surroundings is crucial for making informed decisions while driving. Always know what is around you: ahead of you (green zone), next to you (blue zone), in your blind spots (yellow zone), and behind you (red zone). Continuously move your eyes and scan the road at least 10 seconds ahead to anticipate hazards and avoid sudden maneuvers.

Tailgating

Maintain a safe following distance using the three-second rule to keep a safe distance from the vehicle ahead, providing ample time to react if they brake suddenly. If a vehicle merges closely in front of you, take your foot off the accelerator to create space. Increase space when following motorcyclists, on slippery surfaces, or when being tailgated.

Side Awareness and Blind Spots

Avoid driving in another driver's blind spot to prevent sudden lane changes into your path. Keep space between your vehicle and others, especially at intersections, and allow room for merging traffic even if you have the right-of-way. Always check your blind spots by looking over your shoulders before changing lanes, turning, merging, backing up, leaving a parking space, parallel parking, pulling out from the curb, or opening your car door.

Rear Awareness

Regularly use rearview and side mirrors to check for traffic behind you, especially when changing lanes, reducing speed, turning, stopping, or backing up.

Speed Management

Adhere to the basic speed law: drive no faster than is safe for current road conditions, regardless of the posted speed limit. Adjust your speed considering traffic, road surface, weather, and the presence of pedestrians or bicyclists. The ideal maximum speed limit on most California highways is 65 mph, 55 mph on a two-lane undivided highway, and lower for vehicles towing trailers.

Handling Hazards

When faced with multiple hazards, prioritize avoiding the more dangerous one. For instance, if there is oncoming traffic and a bicyclist, let the oncoming traffic pass before moving left to pass the bicyclist safely.

Distractions and Technology

Avoid engaging in activities that divert your attention from driving, such as using a phone, changing music, or applying makeup. Use cell phones only in hands-free mode. Minors are prohibited from using cell phones while driving, except in emergencies. Stay updated on new vehicle technologies, including advanced driver assistance systems (ADAS) and self-driving features.

Carbon Monoxide Awareness

Prevent carbon monoxide poisoning by never starting your vehicle in a closed garage. Be aware of symptoms such as tiredness, dizziness, nausea, and headaches.

Emergencies
Tire Blowout

In the event of a tire blowout, hold the steering wheel firmly, maintain speed, gradually release the accelerator, stabilize the vehicle, and then slow down and pull off the road safely.

Driving Off Pavement

If you drive off the pavement, grip the steering wheel firmly, remove your foot from the accelerator, brake gently, check for traffic behind, and carefully steer back onto the pavement.

Overheating

Monitor the temperature gauge, avoid high speeds, and turn off the air conditioner in extreme heat to prevent the vehicle from overheating.

Disabled Vehicles

If your vehicle becomes disabled, safely pull over, use emergency flashers, and call for assistance if needed. Stay inside the vehicle with your seat belt on if possible.

Safety Measures

Seat Belts

Always wear your seat belt correctly, with the shoulder harness across the shoulder and chest, and the lap belt low across the hips. Pregnant women should place the lap belt under the abdomen.

Child Restraints

Children under 2 years old, under 40 pounds, and under 3 feet 4 inches tall must be secured in a rear-facing child passenger restraint system. Children under 8 years old, or less than 4 feet 9 inches tall, should be secured in a child passenger restraint system in a rear seat.

Air Bags

Sit at least 10 inches away from the airbag cover. Ensure children do not sit next to side airbags.

Unattended Children and Pets

Never leave children or pets unattended in a vehicle, especially in hot weather, due to the risk of heatstroke and death.

By following these safe driving practices, you contribute to a safer driving environment for yourself and others on the road. Stay alert, stay focused, and always prioritize safety.

Driving in Different Conditions

Driving in various conditions requires different skills and heightened awareness to ensure safety. This chapter provides essential tips and best practices for handling different environments and weather conditions.

Slippery Roads

Rain, snow, and mud can create slippery conditions. Adjust your driving as follows:

- **Wet Roads:** Reduce speed by 5 to 10 mph.
- **Packed Snow:** Reduce speed by half.
- **Ice:** Reduce speed to no more than 5 mph.

Additional Tips:

- **Shaded Areas:** Be cautious of icy spots in shaded areas.
- **Bridges and Overpasses:** These surfaces freeze first and can be particularly slippery.

- **First Rain:** Roads can be especially slippery at the start of rain due to accumulated oil and dust.

Turn on your windshield wipers, low-beam headlights, and defroster in wet conditions. If visibility is less than 100 feet, do not drive faster than 30 mph.

Skidding

Skidding occurs when your tires lose traction with the road. It can happen on slippery surfaces like ice, snow, or wet pavement.

Slippery Surface Skids:

- **Slow Down:** Reduce speed when approaching intersections and curves.
- **Avoid Quick Stops and Turns:** Make gradual stops and turns to prevent skidding.
- **Use Low Gears on Hills:** Shift to lower gears before going downhill to maintain control.
- **Avoid Hazardous Areas:** Steer clear of ice patches, wet leaves, oil spots, or standing water.

If You Start to Skid:

1. **Remove Foot from Accelerator:** Gradually slow down.
2. **Do Not Brake:** Avoid using the brakes to prevent further loss of control.
3. **Steer in the Direction of the Skid:** Turn the steering wheel in the direction you want the front of the car to go.
4. **Find Dry Pavement:** Try to steer onto dry pavement to regain traction.

Locked Wheel Skids:

- **Four-Wheel ABS:** Apply firm pressure on the brake pedal.
- **Rear-Wheel ABS:** Ease off the brake pedal while maintaining enough pressure to allow the front wheels to roll again.
- **Front-Wheel ABS:** Remove your foot from the brake pedal to unlock the wheels and steer in the desired direction.

If your vehicle lacks ABS, pump the brakes gently to slow down. If the brake pedal sinks to the floor, pump it quickly and downshift to slow down, then use the emergency brake.

Stuck in Snow or Mud

If you get stuck, follow these steps:

1. Shift into low gear and keep the wheels straight.
2. Gently step on the accelerator to avoid spinning the wheels.

3. Drive forward as far as possible, then shift into reverse and back up.
4. Repeat the forward-backward motion until free.
5. Place boards or branches under the tires for traction if needed.

Hydroplaning

Hydroplaning occurs when your vehicle rides on water, losing contact with the road. To avoid hydroplaning:

- **Drive Slowly:** Reduce speed in wet conditions.
- **Steer Around Standing Water:** Avoid driving through large puddles.
- **Listen for Sloshing Sounds:** If you hear sloshing, slow down.
- **Gradual Speed Reduction:** If you start to hydroplane, ease off the accelerator and steer straight until you regain control. Do not brake suddenly.

Driving in Darkness

Driving at night presents unique challenges due to reduced visibility. Follow these guidelines to navigate safely in the dark:

- **Use High-Beam Headlights:** On open country roads or dark city streets, use your high-beam headlights. Ensure you can stop within the illuminated area. Dim your high beams for oncoming traffic to avoid blinding other drivers.
- **Avoid Direct Headlight Glare:** If another vehicle's lights are too bright, do not look directly at them. Instead, focus on the right edge of your lane and watch the oncoming vehicle out of the corner of your eye.
- **Nighttime Awareness:** Be extra cautious of motorcycles, pedestrians, and bicyclists, who are harder to see. Slow down in highway construction zones and adjust your speed when leaving brightly lit areas until your eyes adjust to the darkness.

Sun Glare

Sun glare can severely impair your vision, especially during sunrise and sunset. Here are some tips to manage it:

- **Keep Windshields Clean:** Ensure both the inside and outside of your windshield are clean.
- **Use Polarized Sunglasses:** These can help reduce glare.
- **Adjust Car Visors:** Make sure your car visors are in good condition and use them to block the sun.
- **Maintain Safe Distance:** Keep enough space between your vehicle and others to react to sudden stops or changes in traffic.

- **Be Cautious of Pedestrians:** Sun glare can make it difficult to see pedestrians, so be extra vigilant.

Flooded Roads

Flooding can be dangerous. Avoid driving through flooded areas, as it can result in being swept off the road, unseen hazards, road collapse, vehicle malfunction, or electrocution from fallen power lines. If you must drive through a flooded area, proceed slowly and test your brakes afterward to ensure they function correctly.

High Winds

High winds can be particularly hazardous, especially for larger vehicles. Follow these tips:

- **Reduce Speed:** Slower speeds improve control.
- **Firm Hand Position:** Keep a firm grip on the steering wheel.
- **Be Alert for Debris:** Watch for obstacles blown into the roadway.
- **Avoid Cruise Control:** Maintain direct control over your vehicle.
- **Consider Stopping:** If winds are too strong, it may be safer to pull over and wait.

Fog or Heavy Smoke

Driving in fog or heavy smoke is dangerous. Consider postponing your trip, but if you must drive:

- **Drive Slowly:** Reduce speed to match visibility.
- **Use Low-Beam Headlights:** High beams reflect off fog and reduce visibility.
- **Increase Following Distance:** Allow more space between vehicles.
- **Use Windshield Wipers and Defroster:** Maintain clear visibility.
- **Listen for Traffic:** Be aware of vehicles you cannot see.

If the fog becomes too thick, pull off the road, activate emergency flashers, and wait for conditions to improve.

By adapting your driving to these various conditions, you can significantly enhance your safety and the safety of others on the road.

Sharing the Road with Other Vehicles

Driving safely and efficiently involves understanding how to share the road with various types of vehicles. From large trucks and buses to motorcycles, bicycles, and pedestrians, each road user has unique characteristics and requirements. By learning how to navigate around these different vehicles, you can help prevent accidents and ensure a smoother flow of traffic.

Blind Spots (The No Zone)

Large vehicles such as trucks and buses have significant blind spots, often referred to as "The No Zone." These blind spots are areas around the vehicle where the driver cannot see other vehicles. The most substantial blind spots are located directly behind the vehicle and along the sides, especially near the rear wheels. If you cannot see the truck's side mirrors, it means the truck driver cannot see you either. Therefore, avoid lingering in these areas to reduce the risk of accidents. Always make sure to pass through these zones quickly and safely, ensuring you are visible to the driver as much as possible.

Turning

Due to the size and length of large vehicles, their rear wheels follow a shorter path than their front wheels when turning. This means that large vehicles need to swing wide to the left before making a right turn or swing wide to the right before making a left turn. This maneuver is necessary to avoid hitting the curb or other obstacles. As a driver, it is essential to watch for turn signals on large vehicles and anticipate their wide turns. Do not attempt to pass a large vehicle when it is turning, as this can put you in the path of the turning truck and lead to a collision. Always give large vehicles plenty of space to complete their turns safely.

Maneuvering

Large vehicles are less maneuverable than passenger vehicles and typically use the two rightmost lanes on highways with four or more lanes. Avoid:

- Changing lanes directly in front of them.
- Driving alongside them longer than necessary; always pass on the left.
- Following too closely.
- Underestimating their size and speed.

Braking

Large vehicles need more distance to stop than passenger vehicles. At 55 mph, a passenger vehicle can stop within 300 feet, but a large vehicle might need up to 400 feet. Avoid cutting in front of large vehicles and stopping suddenly.

Buses, Streetcars, and Trolleys

Safety zones are for pedestrians waiting for buses, streetcars, and trolleys, marked by raised buttons or markers. Do not drive through a safety zone. When passing a stopped bus, streetcar, or trolley, do not exceed 10 mph. Pass light rail vehicles or streetcars on the left only if necessary.

Light Rail Vehicles

Light rail vehicles have the same rights as other vehicles. To share the road safely:

- Be aware of their routes and potential blind spots.
- Never turn in front of an approaching light rail vehicle.
- Maintain a safe distance.
- Check for light rail vehicles before turning across tracks.

Motorcycles

Motorcyclists have the same rights and responsibilities as other drivers. To share the road safely:

- Check for motorcycles when changing lanes or entering a road.
- Allow a three-second following distance.
- Give a motorcycle the full lane when possible.
- Check for motorcyclists before opening your door.
- Move to one side of your lane to give motorcyclists room to pass.

Emergency Vehicles

Yield to any emergency vehicle using a siren and red lights by driving to the right edge of the road and stopping until the vehicle has passed. Continue through an intersection if you see an emergency vehicle, then pull to the right and stop. Obey directions from law enforcement or firefighters, even if they conflict with existing signs or laws. Do not follow an emergency vehicle within 300 feet or drive to the scene of a disaster.

Slow-moving Vehicles

These vehicles take longer to accelerate and may slow down on hills. They often display an orange and red triangle and travel at 25 mph or less. Adjust your speed to share the road safely.

Neighborhood Electric Vehicles (NEVs) and Low-speed Vehicles (LSVs)

NEVs and LSVs are types of slow-moving vehicles, typically limited to a maximum speed of 25 mph. They are commonly used for short trips within residential areas or urban environments. Look out for signs such as "NEV USE ONLY" or "NEV ROUTE," which indicate areas where these vehicles are permitted. Because of their speed limitations, NEVs and LSVs are restricted from traveling on roads where the speed limit exceeds 35 mph to ensure safety.

Animal-drawn Vehicles

Horse-drawn vehicles and riders on horses or other animals share the road with motor vehicles. Drivers should be cautious and respectful when encountering these vehicles. It is illegal to intentionally scare horses or livestock, as doing so could cause accidents or harm to both the animals and humans involved. Always give animal-drawn vehicles plenty of space and proceed slowly to avoid startling the animals.

Near Animals

When you see road signs depicting animals, it indicates that animals might be on or near the road. This is common in rural areas or places near wildlife habitats. If you encounter animals or livestock near the road, slow down or stop to avoid a collision. Always follow any instructions given by the person in charge of the animals, who may need to move them across or along the roadway.

Bicycles

Bicyclists have the same rights and responsibilities as motor vehicle drivers. Here are some key points to remember:

- **Legally riding on freeways**: Bicyclists may ride on certain freeway sections where there are no alternate routes, provided bicycling is not prohibited.
- **Avoiding hazards**: Bicyclists may move left to avoid hazards like parked cars, moving vehicles, animals, or debris.
- **Left curb on one-way streets**: Bicyclists can ride near the left curb or edge of a one-way street.
- **Using crosswalks**: Bicyclists may use crosswalks by stopping and crossing as a pedestrian.

Bicyclist Responsibilities

As a bicyclist, you must follow these rules:

- **Obey traffic signs and signals**: Just like motor vehicles, bicyclists must obey all traffic signs, signal lights, and basic right-of-way rules.
- **Ride with traffic**: Always ride in the same direction as traffic to ensure visibility and predictability.
- **Check before turning**: Always look over your shoulder to make sure the lane is clear before turning or changing lanes.
- **Turn like drivers**: Make left and right turns in the same way drivers do, using hand signals and turn lanes.
- **Use bike lanes**: Whenever possible, use designated bike lanes or the through traffic lane.
- **Functional brakes**: Ensure your bicycle is equipped with fully functional brakes.
- **Yield to pedestrians**: Pedestrians have the right-of-way.
- **Wear a helmet**: If you are under 18, wearing a helmet is mandatory.
- **Stay visible**: Avoid weaving between parked vehicles and stay as visible as possible.
- **Ride near the right curb**: Ride as close to the right curb or edge of the roadway as possible.
- **Sidewalk rules**: Do not ride on the sidewalk unless permitted by local regulations.

Bicycling at Night

Visibility is crucial when bicycling at night. Avoid wearing dark clothing, and make sure your bicycle has the following equipment:

- **Front lamp**: A white light visible from 300 feet.
- **Rear red reflector or light**: Visible from 500 feet.
- **Pedal reflectors**: White or yellow reflectors on each pedal, your shoes, or your ankles, visible from 200 feet.
- **Wheel reflectors**: White or yellow reflectors on the front wheel and a white or red reflector on the rear wheel, or reflectorized tires.

Bicycling in Travel Lanes

Bicyclists traveling slower than traffic must ride as close as possible to the right curb or edge of the road, unless:

- **Passing**: Passing another vehicle or bicycle in the same direction.
- **Turning left**: Preparing to make a left turn.
- **Narrow lanes**: The lane is too narrow for a bicycle and a vehicle to travel safely side-by-side.
- **Approaching a right turn**: Approaching a right turn.
- **One-way roads**: On one-way roads with two or more lanes, bicyclists may ride near the left curb or edge.
- **Avoiding hazards**: Avoiding obstacles or hazardous road conditions.

Drivers should maintain a safe following distance. When safe, the bicyclist should move to allow vehicles to pass.

Passing a Bicyclist

To pass a bicyclist safely:

- **Change lanes if necessary**: Leave sufficient space between your vehicle and the bicyclist.
- **Maintain a safe distance**: Allow at least three feet between your vehicle and the bicyclist. If you cannot provide this space, wait until it is safe to pass.
- **Avoid forcing the bicyclist**: Ensure bicyclists are not forced into parked vehicles or open doors.
- **Merge carefully**: Merge toward the curb or into the bike lane only when it is safe.
- **Turn preparation**: Merge safely behind a bicyclist when preparing to turn.
- **Bike lane usage**: Enter a bike lane no more than 200 feet before starting a turn.
- **Check for bicyclists**: When changing lanes or entering traffic, check for bicyclists who may be in blind spots.
- **Two-lane roads**: Be cautious when approaching or passing a bicyclist.

Road Workers and Work Zones

When approaching work zones, you will see warning signs and message boards indicating the presence of workers, slow-moving equipment, and closed lanes. Navigate these areas safely by:

- **Slowing down**: Reduce your speed.
- **Allowing extra space**: Maintain extra space between vehicles.
- **Expecting sudden stops**: Anticipate sudden slowing or stopping.
- **Watching for lane changes**: Be alert for drivers changing lanes.
- **Avoiding distractions**: Stay focused and avoid distractions.

Cones, drums, or barriers will guide you through the work zone. Prepare to slow down or stop for highway equipment and merge safely without crossing cones or drums. Watch for bicycles if lanes are narrow or the shoulder is closed. Obey special signs or instructions from workers, such as flaggers.

Move Over and Slow Down

Drivers must move over and slow down for stationary emergency and road work vehicles displaying flashing amber warning lights.

Vehicles with Hazardous Loads

Trucks carrying hazardous materials, marked with a diamond-shaped sign, must stop before crossing railroad tracks to ensure safety.

Heavy Traffic or Bad Weather

In heavy traffic or bad weather, drive slower, but do not obstruct normal traffic flow. If you drive faster or slower than the speed limit, you may be cited. Move to the right if another driver wishes to pass. If you drive slower than other traffic, stay in the right lane.

Towing

When towing a vehicle or trailer, drive in the far-right lane or a lane designated for slower vehicles. If no lanes are marked and there are four or more lanes, use the two rightmost lanes.

Around Children

The speed limit is 25 mph within 500 feet of a school when children are outside or crossing the street. Some school zones have limits as low as 15 mph. Near schools, look for:

- **Bicyclists and pedestrians**: Be cautious of children on bicycles and on foot.
- **School safety patrols or crossing guards**: Always obey their directions.
- **Stopped school buses**: Watch for children crossing the street.

When a school bus flashes yellow lights, it is preparing to stop. Slow down and prepare to stop. When the bus flashes red lights, you must stop from either direction until the children are safely across the street and the lights stop flashing. Failing to stop can result in a fine up to $1,000 and a one-year suspension of driving privileges. You do not need to stop if the bus is on the opposite side of a divided highway.

Blind Intersections

A blind intersection has no stop signs and visibility is obstructed. If you cannot see 100 feet in either direction during the last 100 feet before crossing, it is considered blind. Move slowly forward until you can see. The speed limit for a blind intersection is 15 mph.

Alleys

An alley is a narrow road, no wider than 25 feet, used to access the rear or side entrances of buildings. You may drive on or cross a sidewalk to enter or exit a driveway or alley. The speed limit in an alley is 15 mph.

Near Railroad or Light Rail Tracks

The speed limit is 15 mph within 100 feet of a railroad crossing if visibility is limited to 400 feet in both directions. You may drive faster if the crossing is controlled by gates, a warning signal, or a flagman. At railroad crossings:

- **Flashing red warning lights**: Stop and wait. Do not proceed until the lights stop flashing, even if the gate rises.
- **Approaching trains**: Stop at least 15 feet from the nearest track when warned of an approaching train.
- **Crossing gates**: Do not go under or around lowering gates. If gates are down and no train is visible, call the posted emergency number or 911.
- **Stop, look, and listen**: Do not cross if a train is coming or a horn or bell sounds. Many crossings have multiple tracks; look both ways and cross only when safe.
- **Never stop on tracks**: Ensure you have enough room to cross completely. If on the tracks, you risk injury or death.
- **Watch for stopping vehicles**: Buses, school buses, and vehicles with hazardous material placards must

Business or Residential Districts The speed limit is 25 mph unless otherwise posted.

Fines and Double Fine Zones

Traffic violations in work zones can result in fines of $1,000 or more. Assaulting a highway worker can lead to fines up to $2,000 and imprisonment for up to one year. Some roads are designated as Safety Enhanced-Double Fine Zones due to increased collision-related injuries and fatalities, where fines are doubled. Fines are also doubled in highway construction or maintenance zones when workers are present.

Chapter VII: Legal Responsibilities

Changing, Replacing, and Renewing Your Driver's License

Keeping your driver's license up to date is crucial for legal driving and ensuring your personal information remains current with the DMV. Here's what you need to know about changing, replacing, and renewing your driver's license.

Changing Your Driver's License Information

If you need to update your personal information on your driver's license, such as your name or address, you must notify the DMV within 10 days.

1. **Change of Address:**
   o You can update your address online at the DMV website, by mail, or in person at a DMV office. Visit dmv.ca.gov/addresschange for the online form.
   o Complete a Change of Address form (DMV 14) and submit it.
   o A new physical driver's license with your updated address will not be issued automatically. However, you can request a replacement license with your new address for a fee.
2. **Change of Name:**
   o To change your name on your driver's license, visit a DMV office in person.
   o Bring legal documentation of your name change, such as a marriage certificate, divorce decree, or court order.
   o Complete a Driver's License or Identification Card Application (Form DL 44).
   o Pay the applicable fee for a new driver's license with your updated name.

Replacing a Lost, Stolen, or Damaged Driver's License

If your driver's license is lost, stolen, or damaged, you need to apply for a replacement as soon as possible.

1. **Application Process:**
   o You can apply for a replacement online, by mail, or in person at a DMV office. Visit dmv.ca.gov/dlservices for more information.
   o Complete a Driver's License or Identification Card Application (Form DL 44).
   o Pay the required replacement fee.
2. **Identity Verification:**
   o Provide proof of identity, such as a birth certificate, passport, or other DMV-approved documents.
   o If applying in person, bring these documents with you. If applying online or by mail, be prepared to upload or send copies.

3. **Temporary License:**
    o A temporary driver's license may be issued if you apply in person, which is valid until you receive your replacement license by mail.

Renewing Your Driver's License

Driver's licenses in California must be renewed every five years. It is illegal to drive with an expired driver's license. The DMV sends a renewal notice about 60 days before your license expires. Here's how to renew your driver's license:

1. **Renewal Methods:**
    o You can renew your driver's license online, by mail, or in person at a DMV office. Visit dmv.ca.gov/dlservices for more information.
2. **Complete the Renewal Application:**
    o Fill out the Driver's License or Identification Card Application (Form DL 44).
3. **Pay the Renewal Fee:**
    o Pay the applicable renewal fee using a credit card, debit card, check, or money order.
4. **Required Tests and Documentation:**
    o If you are 70 years old or older, you must renew your driver's license in person and pass a vision test. The DMV may also require a knowledge test.
    o If you have certain medical conditions or your driving record requires it, you may be asked to take additional tests.
    o If your driver's license and identity document (e.g., passport) expire on the same date, you will need to provide a valid identity document.
5. **Receive Your New License:**
    o Once processed, your new driver's license will be mailed to you. If you renewed in person, you will receive a temporary license valid until your new one arrives.

Extending Your Driver's License

If you are out-of-state and cannot renew your driver's license before it expires, you may request a one-year extension.

1. **Eligibility:**
    o Limited-term driver's licenses are not eligible for this extension.
2. **Application Process:**
    o Before your driver's license expires, submit a request with your name, driver's license number, birth date, California residence address, and out-of-state address to dl-extensions@dmv.ca.gov.

Alcohol and Driving

Driving under the influence of alcohol or drugs is illegal and poses significant risks. California's DUI laws apply to both alcohol and drugs, including prescription and over-the-counter medications that impair driving ability. Here are key points you need to know:

Legal Limits and Penalties:

- It is illegal to drive with a blood alcohol concentration (BAC) of 0.08% or higher if you are over 21, 0.04% or higher if you are driving a commercial vehicle, and 0.01% or higher if you are under 21 or on DUI probation.
- DUI penalties include fines, license suspension, mandatory DUI education programs, and possible jail time. Repeated offenses result in harsher penalties.

DUI Laws for All Ages:

- It is illegal to drive after consuming excessive amounts of alcohol or any drug that impairs your ability to drive, including medications like cough syrup.
- Make sure to read medication labels and understand the effects of any drug you use.

Open Container Laws:

- It is illegal to have an open container of alcohol or cannabis products in the passenger area of a vehicle. These must be stored in the trunk or an area not accessible to the driver and passengers.

Sobriety Tests and Refusals:

- Law enforcement officers can ask you to take a breath, blood, or urine test if they suspect DUI. Refusing these tests can result in immediate license suspension for one year.

DUI Arrests and Convictions:

- Upon arrest for DUI, California's Administrative Per Se law requires DMV to suspend your driving privilege.
- You may receive a temporary driver's license valid for 30 days, and you can request a DMV administrative hearing within 10 days from the date of your arrest.
- If convicted, your driving privilege will be suspended or revoked, and you must complete a DUI program, file SR 22/SR 1P, pay applicable fees, and possibly install an ignition interlock device (IID).
- DUI convictions remain on your record for 10 years, and repeat offenses within this period result in increased penalties.

Drivers Under 21:

- Additional laws prohibit drivers under 21 from carrying alcohol in a vehicle unless accompanied by someone 21 or older, and the container must be unopened. Violations can result in vehicle impoundment, fines, and license suspension.
- Underage drivers with a BAC of 0.01% or higher face a one-year license suspension and must complete a licensed DUI program.

Safety Measures and Avoidance:

- Plan ahead if you intend to drink by using a designated driver, public transportation, or ride-sharing services.
- Understand that even small amounts of alcohol can impair your driving abilities.

Use or Possession of Alcohol or Cannabis Products in a Vehicle:

- It is illegal to drink alcohol or use cannabis products while driving or riding as a passenger. Open containers must be kept in the trunk or an area not accessible to passengers.
- This law does not apply to passengers in buses, taxis, campers, or motorhomes.

Blood Alcohol Concentration (BAC) Limits:

- BAC measures the amount of alcohol in your bloodstream. Legal limits vary: 0.08% for drivers over 21, 0.01% for drivers under 21 or on DUI probation, and 0.04% for commercial drivers or drivers for hire.
- Even if your BAC is below legal limits, you can still be charged with DUI if you are impaired.

Number of Drinks	M/F	Body Weight in Pounds								Driving Condition
		100	120	140	160	180	200	220	240	
0	M	.00	.00	.00	.00	.00	.00	.00	.00	Only Safe Driving Limit
	F	.00	.00	.00	.00	.00	.00	.00	.00	
1	M	.06	.05	.04	.04	.03	.03	.03	.02	Driving Skills Impaired
	F	.07	.06	.05	.04	.04	.03	.03	.03	
2	M	.12	.10	.09	.07	.07	.06	.05	.05	
	F	.13	.11	.09	.08	.07	.07	.06	.06	
3	M	.18	.15	.13	.11	.10	.09	.08	.07	
	F	.20	.17	.14	.12	.11	.10	.09	.08	Legally Intoxicated
4	M	.24	.20	.17	.15	.13	.12	.11	.10	
	F	.26	.22	.19	.17	.15	.13	.12	.11	
5	M	.30	.25	.21	.19	.17	.15	.14	.12	
	F	.33	.28	.24	.21	.18	.17	.15	.14	

BLOOD ALCOHOL CONTENT (BAC)
Table for Male (M) / Female (F)

Subtract .01% for each 40 minutes that lapse between drinks.
1 drink = 1.5 oz. 80 proof liquor, 12 oz. 5% beer, or 5 oz. 12% wine.
Fewer than 5 persons out of 100 will exceed these values.

Insurance

Having valid auto insurance is a legal requirement for all drivers. Insurance helps cover costs in the event of an accident, protecting you, your passengers, and other road users. Here are the key points you need to know about insurance requirements in California:

Minimum Insurance Coverage: Your insurance policy must meet the following minimum liability coverage limits:

- $15,000 for injury or death to one person.
- $30,000 for injury or death to more than one person.
- $5,000 for property damage.

Proof of Insurance: You must carry proof of insurance in your vehicle at all times. This proof must be shown to law enforcement officers upon request, during a drive test, and to other drivers involved in a collision. Acceptable forms of proof include an insurance card, electronic proof on your smartphone, or other documentation provided by your insurer.

Parental Responsibility: Parents or guardians are financially responsible for drivers under 18 years old and must pay for damages if the young driver is involved in a collision. Drivers 18 years and older are responsible for their own financial liability.

Low-Cost Insurance: If you cannot afford standard liability insurance, you may be eligible for the California Low Cost Automobile Insurance Program. For more information, visit mylowcostauto.com or call 1-866-602-8861.

Before Purchasing Insurance: Ensure that the agent, broker, or insurance provider is licensed by the California Department of Insurance. You can verify this by visiting insurance.ca.gov/license-status/.

Collisions

Understanding the common causes of collisions and knowing what to do if you are involved in one can help you stay safe and comply with legal requirements.

Causes of Collisions: The most common causes of collisions include:

- Driver distractions.
- Unsafe speed.
- Improper turns.
- Not following the right-of-way rules.
- Ignoring stop signals and signs.
- Driving on the wrong side of the road.
- Traveling significantly faster or slower than the flow of traffic.

What to Do if You Are in a Collision:

1. **Stop Immediately:** You must stop at the scene of the collision. Failing to stop can result in severe penalties, including being charged with a hit-and-run.
2. **Call 911:** If anyone is injured, call 911 immediately for medical assistance. If no one is injured, move your vehicle out of traffic and then call 911.
3. **Exchange Information:** Provide your driver's license, vehicle registration card, insurance information, and current address to the other driver, law enforcement officer, and anyone else involved in the collision.
4. **Report the Collision:** You must report the collision to law enforcement within 24 hours if anyone is injured or killed. Your insurance agent, broker, or legal representative can file the report for you.
5. **Notify the Owner:** If you hit a parked car or other property, try to find the owner. If you cannot, leave a note with your name, phone number, and address securely attached to the vehicle or property and report the collision to law enforcement.
6. **Injured Animals:** If you injure an animal, call the nearest humane society or law enforcement. Do not attempt to move the animal yourself.

Reporting a Collision: You must report a collision to the DMV within 10 days if:

- The collision caused more than $1,000 in property damage.
- Anyone was injured or killed, even if the injuries were minor.

Each driver involved in such a collision must file a Report of Traffic Accident Occurring in California (SR 1) with the DMV. You must file this report whether or not you were at fault, and even if the collision occurred on private property. Failure to report the collision can result in suspension of your driving privilege.

Driving Without Insurance

If you are involved in a collision and do not have proper insurance coverage, your driving privilege will be suspended for up to four years, regardless of who was at fault. You may regain your driver's license during the last three years of the suspension period by providing a California Insurance Proof Certificate (SR 22/SR 1P) and maintaining it for the remainder of the suspension period.

Collisions on Your Driver's Record

Any collision resulting in over $1,000 in damage, injury, or death must be reported to the DMV, which will add the incident to your driver's record. This is true regardless of who caused the collision.

By understanding and adhering to these insurance requirements and procedures, you can ensure that you are financially protected and compliant with California laws, thereby contributing to safer roadways for everyone.

Vehicle Registration

Registering your vehicle is a legal requirement in California, ensuring that your vehicle is recognized by the state and is in compliance with safety and environmental standards. Here's what you need to know about vehicle registration:

Initial Registration

When you purchase a new or used vehicle, you must register it with the California Department of Motor Vehicles (DMV). Here are the steps for initial registration:

1. **Obtain the Required Documents:**
   - **Proof of Ownership:** If you purchased a new vehicle, you will need the Manufacturer's Certificate of Origin. For a used vehicle, you will need the title signed over to you by the previous owner.
   - **Bill of Sale:** This is necessary to prove the purchase price and date of purchase.
   - **Smog Certificate:** Required for vehicles that are more than four years old and less than ten years old. Vehicles older than ten years may need additional testing.

- o **Vehicle/Vessel Transfer and Reassignment Form (REG 262):** Needed for vehicles that are leased or have a lienholder. This form must be completed and signed.
2. **Complete the Application:**
   - o Fill out the Application for Title or Registration (Form REG 343).
   - o If the vehicle is leased, ensure you also complete the REG 656, Lease Agreement.
3. **Pay the Fees:**
   - o Registration fees include title fees, vehicle license fees, county/district fees, and smog fees, if applicable. Use the DMV's fee calculator to estimate your costs.
4. **Submit the Documents and Payment:**
   - o Submit your documents and payment to a DMV office. You may need to schedule an appointment to avoid long wait times.
5. **Receive Your Registration:**
   - o Once processed, you will receive your registration card, license plates, and stickers. Ensure the stickers are affixed to the license plates as instructed.

Renewal of Registration

Vehicle registration must be renewed annually. The DMV will send you a renewal notice about 60 days before your registration expires. Here's how to renew your registration:

1. **Receive the Renewal Notice:**
   - o Check the renewal notice for the amount due and any additional requirements, such as a smog inspection.
2. **Complete Required Inspections:**
   - o If a smog check is required, complete it at a certified smog check station.
3. **Pay the Renewal Fees:**
   - o Pay the required fees online, by mail, or in person at a DMV office.
4. **Receive Your Renewal Materials:**
   - o Upon payment, you will receive your new registration card and stickers. Place the stickers on your license plates as indicated.

Temporary Operating Permits

If your registration has expired and you are unable to complete the renewal process immediately, you may apply for a Temporary Operating Permit (TOP) to avoid penalties and continue driving legally.

1. **Eligibility:**
   - o You may be eligible for a TOP if you need to complete a smog inspection or if you are awaiting documentation to complete the registration process.
2. **Application:**
   - o Visit a DMV office to apply for a TOP. You will need to provide proof of insurance and pay a fee.
3. **Validity:**

- A TOP is typically valid for a limited period, allowing you time to complete the necessary steps for full registration.

Special Situations

Out-of-State Vehicles:

- If you move to California or purchase a vehicle from another state, you must register the vehicle within 20 days. This process includes a smog inspection and verifying the vehicle identification number (VIN).

Non-Operational Vehicles:

- If your vehicle will not be operated or parked on public roads, you can file for a Planned Non-Operation (PNO) status to avoid paying full registration fees. You must file for PNO status before your current registration expires.

Lost or Damaged Registration:

- If your registration card, license plates, or stickers are lost, stolen, or damaged, you must apply for replacements through the DMV. Complete the appropriate forms and pay the replacement fees.

Assessing and Improving Your Driving Skills

Every driver will eventually need to evaluate their driving skills to ensure they are still safe on the road. If you are concerned about your driving abilities, consider asking a trusted individual with a valid driver's license to observe your driving from the passenger seat. Your observer should take note of any dangerous driving behaviors and provide constructive feedback. Listening carefully to these suggestions and applying them can help improve your driving. Professional driving lessons or classes are also valuable options for enhancing your skills.

Conditions Affecting Driving

Cognitive disorders such as dementia, seizure disorders, brain tumors, Parkinson's disease, strokes, or vertigo can significantly impair safe driving abilities. When the DMV receives a referral or diagnosis indicating mild cognitive impairment, the Driver Safety team will schedule a reexamination to assess the driver's capabilities.

Reexamination Process

The California Vehicle Code allows the DMV to investigate and reexamine any driver's ability to operate a motor vehicle safely. This process can be triggered by a physical or mental condition or a poor driving record, not by the driver's age. Drivers with certain conditions can be referred to the DMV by a physician, law enforcement officer, or family member through a completed Request for Driver Reexamination form.

DMV Reexamination Procedures

During a reexamination, the DMV may undertake several actions to assess your driving capabilities:

- Perform an in-person or telephone reexamination.
- Gather medical information from you or your doctor.
- Mandate that you complete knowledge, vision, or driving tests.
- Grant a limited-term driver's license.
- Immediately suspend or revoke your driving privilege if your condition presents an immediate risk to public safety.
- Decide to take no action if your condition does not compromise driving safety.

Priority Reexamination

If law enforcement issues you a Notice of Priority Reexamination, indicated by a check mark in the top box, you must contact the DMV within five working days to initiate the reexamination process. Failure to do so will result in the automatic suspension of your driving privilege.

Possible Driver's License Restrictions

To ensure safe vehicle operation, the DMV may impose the following restrictions on your driver's license:

- Require the use of eyeglasses or corrective lenses.
- Limit driving to specific times or areas, such as prohibiting night or freeway driving.
- Mandate special mechanical devices, such as hand controls.
- Add additional devices, like outside mirrors.

Restrictions are tailored to individual needs and conditions, not age. Any restriction placed on your license is based on the findings and recommendations of a DMV examiner.

By regularly assessing and addressing your driving skills and conditions, you can ensure that you remain a safe and responsible driver on the road.

Chapter VIII: Vehicle Maintenance for Safer Driving

Introduction: Proper vehicle maintenance is crucial for safe driving, optimal performance, and longevity of your vehicle. This chapter will cover essential maintenance tasks, when to seek professional help, and how maintenance contributes to road safety.

Basic Car Maintenance Tips

Regular Oil Changes

- Importance: Ensures proper engine lubrication and prevents wear
- Frequency: Typically every 3,000-7,500 miles, or as recommended by your vehicle's manual
- DIY Tip: Check oil level monthly using the dipstick

Tire Maintenance

- Check tire pressure monthly and before long trips
- Rotate tires every 5,000-8,000 miles
- Replace tires when tread depth is less than 2/32 of an inch
- DIY Tip: Use a penny to check tread depth - if you can see all of Lincoln's head, it's time for new tires

Brake System

- Listen for squealing or grinding noises
- Pay attention to brake pedal feel
- Have brake pads inspected regularly
- DIY Tip: Visually inspect brake pads through wheel spokes

Battery Care

- Keep battery terminals clean
- Ensure connections are tight
- Replace battery every 3-5 years
- DIY Tip: Check for corrosion on terminals and clean with a mixture of baking soda and water

Fluid Levels

- Regularly check and top up:
    - Engine oil
    - Coolant
    - Power steering fluid
    - Brake fluid

      o   Windshield washer fluid
- DIY Tip: Learn the location of fluid reservoirs in your vehicle

Air Filter

- Replace every 15,000-30,000 miles
- More frequently if driving in dusty conditions
- DIY Tip: Hold filter up to a bright light; if you can't see light through it, it needs replacement

Windshield Wipers

- Replace when streaking or skipping
- Typically every 6-12 months
- DIY Tip: Clean wiper blades monthly with windshield washer fluid

Lights

- Check all exterior lights monthly
- Replace burnt-out bulbs promptly
- DIY Tip: Test lights at night against a wall to check alignment

When to Seek Professional Mechanical Help

While many maintenance tasks can be done at home, some require professional expertise:

a) Check Engine Light

- If illuminated, have a professional diagnose the issue promptly

b) Transmission Issues

- Grinding noises, slipping gears, or delayed engagement require expert attention

c) Steering and Suspension

- Unusual noises when turning or going over bumps
- Car pulls to one side while driving

d) Coolant System

- Overheating issues or coolant leaks

e) Timing Belt Replacement

- As per manufacturer's recommendation, typically between 60,000-100,000 miles

f) Major Services

- Follow your vehicle's recommended service schedule for comprehensive check-ups

How Maintenance Contributes to Road Safety

a) Brakes: Well-maintained brakes ensure shorter stopping distances and better control

b) Tires: Proper inflation and good tread depth improve traction and handling

c) Lights: Functioning lights ensure visibility and proper signaling

d) Windshield: Clear visibility is crucial for safe driving

e) Steering and Suspension: Proper alignment and shock absorption contribute to vehicle stability

f) Engine: A well-maintained engine is less likely to break down, reducing the risk of roadside emergencies

Maintenance Records

Keep a log of all maintenance performed on your vehicle. This helps you:

- Track when services are due
- Maintain warranty coverage
- Provide documentation if you sell the vehicle

5. Emergency Kit

Prepare an emergency kit to keep in your vehicle:

- Flashlight and extra batteries
- Basic tools (screwdriver, pliers, wrench)
- Jumper cables
- Flares or reflective triangles
- First-aid kit
- Blanket
- Water and non-perishable snacks

Pro Tips:

1. Read your vehicle's owner's manual thoroughly to understand specific maintenance requirements
2. Address small issues promptly to prevent them from becoming major problems
3. Find a trusted mechanic or dealership for services you can't perform yourself
4. Consider learning basic car maintenance through online tutorials or community classes

Regular vehicle maintenance is an essential aspect of responsible driving. By keeping your vehicle in good condition, you not only ensure your safety but also contribute to the safety of others on the road. Remember, a well-maintained vehicle is more reliable, performs better, and can save you money in the long run by preventing costly repairs. Make vehicle maintenance a priority in your driving routine.

Chapter IX: Legal Updates and Recent Changes

Introduction: California traffic laws are constantly evolving to address new challenges and improve road safety. This chapter covers recent changes and pending legislation that may affect drivers. It's crucial to stay informed about these updates to remain compliant and safe on the road.

New Traffic Laws (Updated for 2024)

1. Automated Speed Enforcement Systems (AB 645) Effective: January 1, 2024 Details: This law authorizes the use of automated speed cameras in certain areas, including school zones and high-injury network streets. Violations captured by these systems may result in civil penalties.

   Key points:

   - Speed cameras will be clearly marked
   - Initial violations result in warnings
   - Subsequent violations incur fines, starting at $50
   - Revenue generated will be used for traffic safety improvements

2. Modified Exhaust Systems (AB 2496) Effective: January 1, 2024 Details: Increases penalties for excessive vehicle noise and modified exhaust systems.

   Key points:

   - First-time offenders may be required to correct the violation
   - Repeat offenders face higher fines and potential vehicle impoundment

3. "Move Over" Law Expansion (AB 2806) Effective: January 1, 2024 Details: Expands the existing "Move Over" law to include stopped waste service vehicles displaying flashing amber lights.

   Key points:

   - Drivers must move over a lane or slow down when approaching stopped waste service vehicles
   - Applies to all roads, not just freeways

4. Bicycle Omnibus Bill (AB 1909) Effective: January 1, 2024 Details: Introduces several changes to improve bicycle safety and accessibility.

   Key points:

   - Allows bicyclists to cross on "Walk" pedestrian signals
   - Prohibits local jurisdictions from requiring bicycle registration
   - Permits e-bikes on certain trails and bikeways unless specifically prohibited

Pending Legislation Affecting Drivers

1. Distracted Driving Prevention Act (SB XXXX) Status: Under consideration Potential impact: Would increase penalties for using handheld devices while driving and expand the definition of distracted driving to include other activities.
2. Zero-Emission Vehicle Mandate (AB YYYY) Status: In committee Potential impact: Would require all new vehicles sold in California to be zero-emission by 2035.
3. Automated Vehicle Testing Expansion (SB ZZZZ) Status: Awaiting vote Potential impact: Would expand areas where companies can test fully autonomous vehicles, potentially increasing their presence on public roads.

How to Stay Informed

1. DMV Website: Regularly check www.dmv.ca.gov for updates on laws and regulations.
2. California Legislative Information: Visit leginfo.legislature.ca.gov for details on pending legislation.
3. Local News: Pay attention to local news outlets for information on new traffic laws.
4. DMV Mailing List: Sign up for the DMV's email updates to receive notifications about important changes.

Laws can change rapidly. Make it a habit to review traffic law updates at least once a year, preferably around January when many new laws take effect.

Chapter X: DMV Resources and Technology

Introduction: The California Department of Motor Vehicles (DMV) has embraced technology to make many of its services more accessible and efficient. This chapter will guide you through the various technological resources available to California drivers, helping you save time and navigate DMV processes more easily.

1. **DMV Website** (www.dmv.ca.gov)

The official DMV website is a comprehensive resource for California drivers. Key features include:

a) Online Services:

- Vehicle registration renewal
- Driver's license renewal
- Change of address
- Appointment scheduling
- Practice tests for learner's permit

b) Forms and Publications:

- Download and print necessary forms
- Access the California Driver Handbook

c) Fee Calculator:

- Estimate fees for various DMV services

Create a DMV online account to access personalized services and save your information for future transactions.

2. **DMV Now Self-Service Terminals**

These convenient kiosks are located at DMV offices, grocery stores, and other public locations.

Services available:

- Vehicle registration renewal
- Print registration card and sticker
- Pay registration fees

How to use:

1. Scan your vehicle registration renewal notice or enter your license plate number and last 5 digits of your VIN
2. Verify your information
3. Pay fees (credit card, debit card, or cash at select locations)
4. Receive your registration card and sticker immediately
5. DMV Mobile App

The official California DMV mobile app offers several convenient features:

- Digital driver's license (pilot program)
- Registration renewal reminders
- Find DMV office locations and wait times
- Access digital DMV Handbook
- Practice tests for learner's permit

Available for both iOS and Android devices.

3. Virtual Field Office

The Virtual Field Office allows you to upload documents and complete certain transactions online that typically require an in-person visit.

Services include:

1. Vehicle title transfers
2. Complex vehicle registration transactions
3. Driver's license reinstatement

4. DMV Chatbot "Miles"

Available on the DMV website, Miles can answer common questions and guide you to the right resources.

5. Social Media Presence

Follow the California DMV on platforms like Twitter, Facebook, and Instagram for:

- Updates on office closures or changes in operations
- New law announcements
- Tips and reminders
- Quick responses to general inquiries

6. DMV Alert Subscription Service

Sign up for email or text alerts about:

- Appointment reminders
- Registration renewal deadlines
- Office closure notifications
- New law updates

7. Interactive Voice Response (IVR) System

Call 1-800-777-0133 to access automated phone services:

- Appointment scheduling
- Office locations and hours
- General information

8. DMV Live Chat

Available on the DMV website during business hours for real-time assistance with general inquiries.

9. Online Driver's Education

The DMV provides links to approved online driver's education courses, allowing new drivers to complete their required education from home.

Pro Tips for Using DMV Technology:

1. Always verify you're using official DMV resources. Be wary of third-party websites that charge unnecessary fees.
2. Keep your DMV online account information secure and up-to-date.
3. Use the DMV website's "Service Advisor" tool to determine the best way to complete your specific transaction.
4. Check for technical issues or scheduled maintenance on the DMV website before planning to use online services.
5. If you're not comfortable with technology, many public libraries offer assistance with accessing online government services.

Conclusion: The California DMV continues to expand its technological offerings to improve service delivery and convenience for drivers. By familiarizing yourself with these resources, you can save time, avoid unnecessary trips to DMV offices, and stay informed about important driving-related matters. Remember, while technology can streamline many processes, some services may still require in-person visits. Always check the DMV website for the most up-to-date information on available services and requirements.

Chapter XI: Practice Tests

Welcome to the Practice Tests section of our California DMV Exam guide. This chapter contains three comprehensive practice tests based on the real California DMV written knowledge exam. These tests are designed to help you assess your understanding of the material covered in this book and prepare you for the actual exam.

As an added bonus, we've provided a QR code. By scanning this code with your smartphone or tablet, or by clicking this link,

https://drive.google.com/drive/folders/1WPw6ScBsxzhIH-np9UL3hbTmHiqsSp7r?usp=sharing
you'll gain access to four additional practice tests, one specifically aimed to sign shape and meaning recognition.

Remember, whether you're using the tests in this book or accessing the downloadale online versions through the QR code, each question is an opportunity to reinforce your knowledge and identify areas that may need further review. Good luck with your studies, and don't forget to scan the QR code for those extra practice tests!

How to Use These Practice Tests:

1. Simulate Real Exam Conditions:
   o Find a quiet place where you won't be interrupted.
   o Set a timer for 45 minutes (the time typically allowed for the actual test).
   o Take the test without referring to the book or other resources.
2. Cover the Answers:
   o Use a blank sheet of paper to cover the answer choices as you read each question.
   o This technique helps prevent your eyes from automatically jumping to the correct answer and forces you to think through each question thoroughly.
3. Answer All Questions:
   o In the real exam, unanswered questions are marked incorrect, so make your best guess if unsure.
4. Review Your Answers:
   o After completing each test, review all answers, including the ones you got correct.
   o Read the explanations provided to deepen your understanding.
5. Track Your Progress:

o   Keep a record of your scores for each practice test.
o   Aim to consistently score 83% or higher (38 out of 46 questions correct) before taking the actual exam.

Tips for Success:

1. Don't Cram: Spread your studying over several days or weeks rather than trying to memorize everything the night before.
2. Focus on Weak Areas: After each practice test, identify topics where you struggled and review those sections in the book.
3. Visualize Scenarios: For questions about traffic situations, try to picture the scenario in your mind.
4. Read Carefully: Pay attention to words like "always," "never," or "unless," which can change the meaning of a question.
5. Stay Calm: If you've prepared well using this guide and these practice tests, you have every reason to feel confident on test day.
6. Get Enough Rest: Ensure you're well-rested before taking the actual exam. A fresh mind performs better.

Remember, these practice tests are tools to help you learn and prepare. Don't be discouraged if you don't score perfectly at first. Each question you get wrong is an opportunity to learn and improve. With diligent study and practice, you'll be well-prepared to ace your California DMV written exam.

PRACTICE TEST 1

Question 1 What procedure should you follow before making a right turn?

1. Slow or stop as necessary before turning
2. Stop, then proceed when clear
3. Signal and turn immediately

Correct Answer: 1

Question 2 When must you comply with instructions from school crossing guards?

1. Only during school hours
2. At all times
3. Unless no children are present

Correct Answer: 2

Question 3 What are the driving privileges with a Class C driver's license?

1. Driving any three-axle vehicle regardless of its weight
2. Driving a vehicle towing two trailers
3. Driving a three-axle vehicle weighing less than 6,000 pounds

Correct Answer: 3

Question 4 To turn left from a multi-lane one-way street to another, you should start from:

1. The lane in the center of the road
2. Any safe lane
3. The lane closest to the left curb

Correct Answer: 3

Question 5 What are your obligations if involved in a traffic collision with significant damage or injuries?

1. Only if you are at fault
2. If there is property damage over $1,000 or any injuries
3. Only if someone is injured

Correct Answer: 2

Question 6 What is the correct procedure for yielding to an emergency vehicle with flashing lights and sirens?

1. Continue driving at the same speed
2. Pull over to the right and stop
3. Speed up to create space

Correct Answer: 2

Question 7 When driving through a roundabout, you should:

1. Yield to traffic already in the roundabout
2. Enter the roundabout without slowing down
3. Stop in the roundabout to check for traffic

Correct Answer: 1

Question 8 When is it appropriate to use your vehicle's hazard lights?

1. When double-parked
2. When your vehicle is disabled on the side of the road
3. When driving in heavy rain

Correct Answer: 2

Question 9 What should you do if your car starts to skid on a slippery road?

1. Brake hard immediately
2. Steer in the direction you want the front wheels to go
3. Speed up to regain traction

Correct Answer: 2

Question 10 How should you react if a driver behind you is tailgating you?

1. Brake suddenly to warn them
2. Speed up to increase the distance
3. Move to another lane or pull over to let them pass

Correct Answer: 3

Question 11 When are roadways most slippery?

1. During a heavy downpour
2. After it has been raining continuously
3. Just after it starts raining following a dry spell

Correct Answer: 3

Question 12 Where is it forbidden to park your vehicle?

1. In emergency situations on the side of a freeway
2. Next to a red-painted curb
3. Within 100 feet of an elementary school

Correct Answer: 2

Question 13 How long should you signal before changing lanes on a freeway?

1. Five seconds
2. Two seconds
3. Four seconds

Correct Answer: 1

Question 14 When is it mandatory to signal before changing lanes?

1. Only when there are other vehicles nearby
2. At all times
3. Only on freeways

Correct Answer: 2

Question 15 What does extending the left arm horizontally from the vehicle indicate?

1. Right turn
2. Left turn
3. Stop

Correct Answer: 2

Question 16 When should you use your horn on narrow mountain roads?

1. To signal to other drivers that you are in a hurry
2. To alert oncoming traffic where you cannot see at least 200 feet ahead

3. To inform pedestrians of your presence

Correct Answer: 2

Question 17 Is it permissible to use your horn in residential areas?

1. Yes, if it's during the day
2. No, unless it's an emergency
3. Only if you reside in the area

Correct Answer: 2

Question 18 When driving at night, you should:

1. Use your high beams at all times
2. Use your low beams in fog, rain, or snow
3. Only use your headlights if there are no streetlights

Correct Answer: 2

Question 19 If an oncoming vehicle is drifting into your lane, you should:

1. Honk your horn and flash your lights
2. Speed up to pass the vehicle quickly
3. Slow down and move to the right if possible

Correct Answer: 3

Question 20 What should you do if your brakes fail while driving?

1. Pump the brakes to build up brake fluid pressure
2. Shift to a higher gear to slow down
3. Immediately pull the parking brake

Correct Answer: 1

Question 21 What equipment is required on a bicycle for night riding to ensure visibility?

1. A white front lamp visible from 300 feet and a rear red reflector or light visible from 500 feet
2. Only a rear red reflector visible from 300 feet
3. Reflective tape on the bicycle frame

Correct Answer: 1

Question 22 When approaching a pedestrian crossing, you should:

1. Speed up to clear the crossing quickly
2. Stop and yield to pedestrians in the crosswalk
3. Continue driving if there are no pedestrians on your side of the road

Correct Answer: 2

Question 23 What is the best action to take if you encounter a large animal on the road?

1. Swerve sharply to avoid hitting it
2. Brake firmly and stay in your lane
3. Speed up to pass it quickly

Correct Answer: 2

Question 24 How can you prevent drowsy driving?

1. Drink caffeinated beverages to stay awake
2. Take regular breaks and get plenty of rest before driving
3. Drive with the windows down to stay alert

Correct Answer: 2

Question 25 What should you do if another driver honks at you?

1. Ignore it and continue driving
2. Make an inappropriate gesture
3. Honk back

Correct Answer: 1

Question 26 When should you activate your headlights?

1. When it's too dark to see from 500 feet away
2. When it's completely dark outside
3. When it's too dark to see from 1000 feet away

Correct Answer: 3

Question 27 Under what conditions is it permissible to drive using only parking lights?

1. 30 minutes after sunset or before sunrise
2. On foggy days
3. It's never permissible

Correct Answer: 3

Question 28 How close should you dim your high beams when approaching or following another vehicle at night?

1. When following within 300 feet of a vehicle
2. When approaching within 500 feet of an oncoming vehicle
3. Both of the above

Correct Answer: 3

Question 29 What should you do when operating your windshield wipers due to fog, rain, or snow?

1. Turn on your low beam headlights
2. Turn on your high beam headlights
3. Activate your emergency flashers

Correct Answer: 1

Question 30 What is the best advice for driving in heavy fog or dust?

1. Alternate using your low and high beams to improve visibility
2. Try not to drive until the conditions improve
3. Don't drive too slowly to avoid being hit from behind

Correct Answer: 2

Question 31 When should you always turn on your headlights on mountain roads and tunnels?

1. Only at night
2. Only on cloudy days
3. Always, regardless of the weather conditions

Correct Answer: 3

Question 32 When is it advisable to tap your brake pedal three or four times?

1. When you need to stop quickly
2. To warn other drivers about a hazard ahead
3. When you want to make a right turn

Correct Answer: 2

Question 33 When is it mandatory to switch from high beams to low beams?

1. Within 300 feet of a vehicle you are following
2. Within 500 feet of an oncoming vehicle
3. In both situations listed above

Correct Answer: 3

Question 34 When is it illegal to drive using only parking lights?

1. At night
2. In residential areas
3. Always

Correct Answer: 3

Question 35 Under what conditions must you turn on your headlights?

1. 30 minutes after sunset and before sunrise
2. Whenever you activate your windshield wipers in adverse weather
3. Both conditions listed above

Correct Answer: 3

Question 36 When should you activate your emergency flashers?

1. To alert other drivers about a collision or hazard ahead
2. When driving on a narrow mountain road
3. When it is raining heavily

Correct Answer: 1

Question 37 This sign on a center lane indicates the lane may be used for:

1. Turning left only
2. Turning left or right
3. Passing slow-moving vehicles

Correct Answer: 1

Question 38 This sign indicates:

1. New lane will be added to the left, merging not required
2. Left lane ends, merge right
3. Passing allowed ahead on the left

Correct Answer: 1

Question 39 This sign at an intersection means:

1. You must yield to oncoming traffic before turning
2. No U-turns are allowed here
3. Stop completely before making a U-turn

Correct Answer: 2

Question 40 This warning sign indicates:

1. Railroad crossing straight ahead
2. Railroad crossing when turning left ahead
3. Railroad crossing when turning right ahead

Correct Answer: 3

Question 41 This traffic sign tells you:

1. The road you are on intersects with a highway ahead
2. Main road curves left with a side road entering from the right
3. Three-way intersection ahead

Correct Answer: 3

Question 42 The sign indicating a narrow bridge ahead means:

1. Soft shoulder warning
2. Narrow bridge ahead
3. Railway tracks ahead

Correct Answer: 2

Question 43 This road sign indicates:

1. Sharp right turn ahead
2. Road joins from the right
3. Road ahead turns sharply right then sharply left

Correct Answer: 3

Question 44 A yellow diamond-shaped sign with an arrow bending to the left means:

1. Left lane ends
2. Merge left
3. Sharp left turn ahead

Correct Answer: 3

Question 45 A yellow sign with a black "+" symbol signifies:

1. Pedestrian crossing
2. Four-way intersection ahead
3. Roundabout ahead

Correct Answer: 2

Question 46 A sign with a truck and a red circle with a slash through it indicates:

1. Truck parking only
2. Truck route ahead
3. No trucks allowed

Correct Answer: 3

PRACTICE TEST 2

Question 1 What is the maximum speed limit on most California highways?

1. 70 mph
2. 65 mph
3. 60 mph

Correct Answer: 2

Question 2 What is the speed limit on two-lane undivided highways unless otherwise posted?

1. 60 mph
2. 55 mph
3. 50 mph

Correct Answer: 2

Question 3 In residential areas, the typical speed limit is:

1. 30 mph
2. 20 mph
3. 25 mph

Correct Answer: 3

Question 4 When driving within 500 to 1,000 feet of a school while children are outside, the speed limit is:

1. 25 mph
2. 20 mph
3. 30 mph

Correct Answer: 1

Question 5 The speed limit in alleys is generally:

1. 20 mph
2. 15 mph
3. 10 mph

Correct Answer: 2

Question 6 What is the speed limit within 100 feet of a railroad crossing where you cannot see the tracks for 400 feet in both directions?

1. 20 mph
2. 10 mph
3. 15 mph

Correct Answer: 3

Question 7 When driving in a business district, the speed limit is usually:

1. 25 mph
2. 20 mph
3. 30 mph

Correct Answer: 1

Question 8 What action should you take when approaching a construction zone with reduced speed limits?

1. Maintain your usual speed
2. Slow down and obey posted signs
3. Speed up to pass quickly

Correct Answer: 2

Question 9 At blind intersections where your view is obstructed, the speed limit is:

1. 20 mph
2. 15 mph
3. 25 mph

Correct Answer: 2

Question 10 If convicted of using alcohol or controlled substances as a minor, the court will:

1. Order the DMV to suspend your license for one year
2. Give you a warning
3. Impose a fine but no license suspension

Correct Answer: 1

Question 11 What must you do if transporting cargo that extends more than 4 feet from the rear bumper of your vehicle?

1. Nothing is required
2. Mark it with a 12-inch red or fluorescent orange square flag during the day and two red lights at night
3. Only secure it with a rope

Correct Answer: 2

Question 12 There are two traffic lanes moving in your direction. You are in the left lane, and many vehicles are passing you on the right. If the driver behind you wishes to drive faster, you should:

1. Stay in your lane so you don't impede the flow of traffic
2. Drive onto the left shoulder to let other vehicles pass
3. Move into the right lane when it is safe

Correct Answer: 3

Question 13 If your vehicle starts to lose traction due to water on the road, you should:

1. Slow down gradually and not apply the brakes
2. Drive at a constant speed to gain better traction
3. Apply the brakes firmly to prevent your vehicle from sliding

Correct Answer: 1

Question 14 In the event of a rear-end collision, you should not:

1. Press your head against the head restraint
2. Brace yourself
3. Release your seat belt

Correct Answer: 3

Question 15 Drivers must use their seat belts:

1. Unless they are driving a limousine
2. And failure to do so will result in a traffic ticket
3. Unless they are driving a vehicle built before 1978

Correct Answer: 2

Question 16 When parking facing uphill on a street with a curb, you should:

1. Leave the front wheels straight
2. Turn the front wheels toward the curb
3. Turn the front wheels away from the curb

Correct Answer: 3

Question 17 Which child requires a child passenger restraint system?

1. A 9-year-old who is 4'10" tall
2. A 10-year-old who is 5'3" tall
3. A 7-year-old who is 4'8" tall

Correct Answer: 3

Question 18 Sudden wind gusts on highways can cause problems for:

1. Only the movement of large vehicles
2. All vehicles
3. Only visibility issues

Correct Answer: 2

Question 19 When is it safe to return to your original lane after passing another vehicle?

1. You can see both headlights of the passed vehicle in your rearview mirror
2. You have cleared the front bumper of the passed vehicle
3. You are 50 ft in front of the passed vehicle

Correct Answer: 1

Question 20 If continually being passed on both sides while driving in the center lane of an expressway, you should:

1. Move to the lane on your right
2. Stay in the center lane
3. Move to the lane on your left

Correct Answer: 1

Question 21 Extra space in front of a large truck is needed for:

1. Other drivers to merge onto the freeway
2. The truck driver to stop the vehicle
3. Other drivers when they want to slow down

Correct Answer: 2

Question 22 On a multi-lane road, a dashed yellow line next to a solid yellow line means:

1. Passing is prohibited from both directions
2. Passing is permitted from both directions
3. Passing is permitted only from the direction next to the dashed line

Correct Answer: 3

Question 23 Always stop before you cross railroad tracks when:

1. You don't have room on the other side to completely cross the tracks
2. The railroad crossing is located in a city or town that has frequent train traffic
3. You transport two or more young children in a passenger vehicle

Correct Answer: 1

Question 24 It is illegal to park your vehicle:

1. Within 3 ft of a private driveway
2. In an unmarked crosswalk
3. In a bicycle lane

Correct Answer: 2

Question 25 When entering the interstate, to merge safely you should:

1. Expect traffic to allow you to proceed into the lane since you have the right of way
2. Merge carefully into the gap
3. Wait for the lane to clear before merging

Correct Answer: 2

Question 26 The speed limit when towing on a two-lane undivided highway is:

1. 55 mph
2. 70 mph

3. 45 mph

Correct Answer: 1

Question 27 If you purchase a vehicle, you must complete the transfer of ownership within:

1. 10 days
2. 20 days
3. 30 days

Correct Answer: 1

Question 28 The correct method to pass large vehicles and trucks is:

1. Always pass a large vehicle on the left side and move ahead of it after passing
2. Pass them quickly on either side without considering their blind spots
3. Pass them on the right side to avoid their blind spots

Correct Answer: 1

Question 29 The proper hand signal for indicating a slowdown or stop is:

1. Hand and arm extended upward
2. Hand and arm extended straight out
3. Hand and arm extended downward

Correct Answer: 3

Question 30 What is the safest way to use a cellular phone while driving?

1. Keep the phone within easy reach
2. Use hands-free devices
3. Check the number before answering

Correct Answer: 2

Question 31 What should you do if the traffic is blocking the intersection despite having a green light?

1. Stay out of the intersection until it clears
2. Enter and wait in the intersection
3. Try to go around the traffic by changing lanes

Correct Answer: 1

Question 32 How should you position your front wheels when parked facing uphill?

1. Facing downhill
2. On a level road
3. Facing uphill

Correct Answer: 3

Question 33 How are school crosswalks typically marked?

1. With white lines
2. With blue lines
3. With yellow crosswalk lines

Correct Answer: 3

Question 34 When is it permissible to use a cellphone without a hands-free device while driving?

1. When stopped at a red light
2. For emergency calls
3. It is never permissible

Correct Answer: 2

Question 35 Which statement accurately reflects the rights and responsibilities of motorcyclists compared to other motorists?

1. Motorcyclists cannot exceed the speed of other traffic during congestion
2. Motorcyclists have equal rights and responsibilities as other motorists
3. Motorcycles are heavier and less affected by adverse weather

Correct Answer: 2

Question 36 Under what circumstances should you always stop before crossing railroad tracks?

1. If the tracks are not in service
2. Whenever a train is approaching, visible or not
3. If your vehicle has three or more axles

Correct Answer: 2

Question 37 This warning sign means:

1.   Winding road begins with a left turn
2.   Passing allowed from both sides
3.   Winding road begins with a right turn

Correct Answer: 1

Question 38 The sign indicating to keep to the right of obstruction signifies:

1.   End of divided highway
2.   Keep right of the obstruction
3.   Left lane ends

Correct Answer: 2

Question 39 This sign indicates:

1.   Side road intersection ahead
2.   Y-intersection ahead
3.   Roadway ends, must turn right or left

Correct Answer: 3

Question 40 This exit speed advisory sign means:

1. Maximum speed is 25 mph under ideal conditions
2. Maximum speed is 25 mph in all conditions
3. Minimum speed limit is 25 mph in all conditions

Correct Answer: 1

Question 41 The sign signifies:

1. End of divided highway ahead
2. Two-way traffic warning ahead
3. Winding road ahead

Correct Answer: 1

Question 42 This sign indicates:

1. Keep to the left, merging traffic ahead
2. Pass on either side of the obstruction
3. Right lane stays to the right, left lane stays to the left

Correct Answer: 2

Question 43 This sign at an intersection means:

1. No right turn allowed at this intersection
2. No right turn on red light
3. All traffic must turn left at the next intersection

Correct Answer: 1

Question 44 This sign indicates:

1. Zoo nearby
2. Deer crossing ahead
3. Wildlife reserve ahead

Correct Answer: 2

Question 45 This sign means:

1. Road narrows ahead
2. Lanes merge to the left
3. Passing allowed in the right lane

Correct Answer: 2

Question 46 This regulatory sign means:

1. No passing zone
2. No parking in this area
3. No pedestrian crossing allowed

Correct Answer: 2

PRACTICE TEST 3

Question 1 What should you do when you encounter a single solid yellow line on your side of the road?

1. Pass the vehicle in front of you
2. Do not pass the vehicle in front of you
3. Drive in the opposite lane

Correct Answer: 2

Question 2 What does a double solid yellow line indicate?

1. Passing is allowed
2. Passing is allowed if you signal
3. Passing is not allowed

Correct Answer: 3

Question 3 When can you legally cross double solid yellow lines?

1. To enter or exit a driveway
2. To overtake a slow-moving vehicle
3. When making a U-turn at any location

Correct Answer: 1

Question 4 What should you do if you see a broken yellow line next to your driving lane?

1. Pass if it is safe
2. Stay in your lane at all times
3. Stop and wait for traffic

Correct Answer: 1

Question 5 What do double solid white lines signify?

1. You can change lanes with caution
2. Do not change lanes
3. You can change lanes anytime

Correct Answer: 2

Question 6 What should you do if your vehicle is being tailgated?

1. Brake suddenly
2. Move to another lane or pull over to let the tailgater pass
3. Speed up to create distance

Correct Answer: 2

Question 7 When driving in heavy fog, which type of headlights should you use?

1. High beam headlights
2. Low beam headlights
3. Emergency flashers

Correct Answer: 2

Question 8 What is the three-second rule used for?

1. Estimating safe following distance
2. Timing traffic lights
3. Calculating stopping distance

Correct Answer: 1

Question 9 How often should you check your mirrors while driving?

1. Every 5 seconds
2. Every 15 seconds
3. Every 2 to 5 seconds

Correct Answer: 3

Question 10 What is the basic speed law?

1. Drive no faster than the posted speed limit
2. Drive no faster than is safe for current conditions
3. Drive at the same speed as other traffic

Correct Answer: 2

Question 11 What should you do if you see a bicyclist ahead and oncoming traffic approaching?

1. Speed up to pass the bicyclist before the oncoming traffic
2. Slow down and let the oncoming traffic pass before passing the bicyclist
3. Honk to alert the bicyclist to move over

Correct Answer: 2

Question 12 For how long should you signal before changing lanes on a freeway?

1. Five seconds
2. Two seconds
3. Four seconds

Correct Answer: 1

Question 13 When must signals be used before changing lanes?

1. Only on freeways
2. At all times
3. Only when other vehicles are nearby

Correct Answer: 2

Question 14 What does extending the left arm horizontally out of the car window indicate?

1. Stopping
2. Turning right
3. Turning left

Correct Answer: 3

Question 15 What should you do when entering a roundabout?

1. Yield to entering traffic
2. Stop in the middle to gauge traffic
3. Yield to traffic already circulating within the roundabout

Correct Answer: 3

Question 16 When is it appropriate to overtake another vehicle?

1. On roads where your lane has a solid line
2. On roads where your lane has a broken line

3. On a hill or curve

Correct Answer: 2

Question 17 At a flashing yellow traffic signal at an intersection, you should:

1. Keep your speed but be mindful of other vehicles
2. Stop completely before crossing
3. Slow down and proceed with caution

Correct Answer: 3

Question 18 What is the speed limit when approaching a railroad crossing with no warning devices and clear visibility of 400 feet?

1. 15 mph
2. 20 mph
3. 25 mph

Correct Answer: 1

Question 19 When parking parallel to the curb on a level street, where should your wheels be positioned?

1. Turned towards the street
2. No more than 18 inches from the curb
3. Touching the curb with one of your rear wheels

Correct Answer: 2

Question 20 What speed should you maintain when merging onto the freeway?

1. At or near the freeway traffic speed
2. Slower than the freeway traffic by 5 to 10 mph
3. At the posted freeway speed limit

Correct Answer: 1

Question 21 In the event of a dust storm impairing visibility, which lights should you turn on while driving slower?

1. Headlights

2. Interior lights
3. Parking lights

Correct Answer: 1

Question 22 What should be your strategy when you decide to overtake another vehicle?

1. Expect the other driver to maintain a steady speed
2. Do not expect the other driver to make space for you
3. Expect the other driver to accommodate you if you signal

Correct Answer: 2

Question 23 What are the requirements for reporting a traffic collision to the DMV?

1. Only if there is property damage over $1,000 or any injuries
2. Only if you or another driver is injured
3. Only if you are at fault

Correct Answer: 1

Question 24 How early should you signal before making a turn?

1. 100 feet
2. 200 feet
3. 50 feet

Correct Answer: 1

Question 25 When must you use your turn signals?

1. When turning left or right
2. When changing lanes or merging
3. In all of the above circumstances

Correct Answer: 3

Question 26 What is the proper sequence for signaling a lane change?

1. Signal, then immediately change lanes
2. Look over your shoulder, signal, then change lanes
3. Change lanes then signal

Correct Answer: 2

Question 27 When are you required to use your hazard lights?

1. When your vehicle is double parked
2. When your vehicle has broken down on the road
3. In heavy rain or fog

Correct Answer: 2

Question 28 When should you deactivate your turn signal?

1. Immediately after completing the turn or lane change
2. Just as you begin the turn or lane change
3. Before you start the turn or lane change

Correct Answer: 1

Question 29 What are the potential consequences of failing to signal when necessary?

1. You may cause an accident
2. You may receive a ticket
3. Both of the above

Correct Answer: 3

Question 30 How should bicyclists indicate their intention to turn?

1. Using their vehicle's signal lights
2. Using specific hand and arm signals
3. Using their horn

Correct Answer: 2

Question 31 Is signaling necessary when moving away from the curb?

1. Only if there are other vehicles around
2. Yes, signaling is necessary
3. No, only when approaching the curb

Correct Answer: 2

Question 32 What action should you take if you find yourself in an intersection and hear an emergency vehicle's siren?

1. Continue, then pull over to the left and stop
2. Continue through, then pull over to the right and stop
3. Stop immediately within the intersection

Correct Answer: 2

Question 33 What is the risk of consistently driving faster and overtaking other vehicles on a one-lane road?

1. It can lead to traffic congestion
2. It can increase the likelihood of accidents
3. It ensures quicker and safer arrival at your destination

Correct Answer: 2

Question 34 Identify the vehicles required to halt before crossing railroad tracks.

1. Any large vehicle such as motorhomes or those towing a trailer
2. Commercial trucks with a visible hazardous material sign
3. Vehicles over 4,000 pounds or with more than three axles

Correct Answer: 2

Question 35 Under what conditions can you make a left turn from one one-way street onto another?

1. If traffic on that street flows to the right
2. If traffic on that street flows to the left
3. Only if there is a sign specifically allowing the turn

Correct Answer: 2

Question 36 How might a large truck behave when turning right into a street with two lanes in each direction?

1. It is restricted to turn within the right lane only
2. It might need to swing wide to successfully make the turn
3. It can turn into either of the two lanes
   Correct Answer: 2

Question 37 A sign with a right arrow and a red circle means:

1. Yield to right turn
2. No right turn
3. Right turn permitted after stop

Correct Answer: 2

Question 38 A white sign with a black "H" and an arrow pointing right indicates:

1. Helipad to the right
2. Hotel to the right
3. Hospital to the right

Correct Answer: 3

Question 39 A yellow sign with a bicycle symbol means:

1. Bicycle lane ends
2. No bicycles allowed
3. **Bicycle crossing**

Correct Answer: 3

Question 40 A sign with a car on a triangle and a wavy line behind it indicates:

1. Road narrows
2. Rough road ahead
3. Slippery road ahead

Correct Answer: 3

Question 41 A sign with a snowflake symbol means:

1. Cold weather ahead
2. Winter driving conditions
3. Snowplow area

Correct Answer: 2

Question 42 A yellow sign with a black arrow pointing left with a red circle means:

1. No left turn
2. Left turn after stop
3. Yield to left turn

Correct Answer: 1

Question 43 A yellow sign with a black arrow curving to the right means:

1. Right lane ends
2. Merge right
3. Sharp right turn

Correct Answer: 3

Question 44 A sign with a car inside a red circle with a line through it means:

1. No vehicles allowed
2. No entry
3. No parking

Correct Answer: 1

Question 45 A yellow diamond-shaped sign with a person on a seesaw indicates:

1. Pedestrian crossing
2. School zone
3. Playground ahead

Correct Answer: 3

Question 46 A yellow sign with a person and a bicycle symbol means:

1. Shared pathway
2. No bicycles allowed
3. Bicycle crossing

Correct Answer: 1

116

Conclusion

Congratulations on completing " The Ultimate California DMV Handbook "! You've taken a significant step towards becoming a knowledgeable and responsible driver in the Golden State. By studying this guide, you've equipped yourself with the essential information needed to pass your California DMV exam and, more importantly, to navigate California's roads safely and confidently.

Remember, the knowledge you've gained here is not just for passing a test—it's the foundation for a lifetime of safe driving. As you transition from studying to practicing behind the wheel, keep in mind the rules, regulations, and safety tips we've covered. Driving is a privilege that comes with great responsibility, and your commitment to being an informed driver contributes to the safety of everyone on the road.

As you prepare to take your DMV exam, remember to stay calm and confident. Trust in the knowledge you've gained, and approach each question with careful consideration. With thorough preparation and a clear mind, you're well-equipped to succeed.

We sincerely wish you the best of luck on your DMV exam and in your future driving endeavors. May your journeys be safe, and may you find joy in the freedom that comes with being a licensed driver in California.

Your Feedback Matters: If you found this guide helpful in your preparation for the DMV exam, we would greatly appreciate your feedback. Please consider leaving a review on Amazon. Your honest review not only helps us improve future editions but also assists other aspiring drivers in finding reliable study resources.

Also you can gain access to the flashcards by clicking this link

https://drive.google.com/drive/folders/1UnEHW-KuqMWZiSGbqnUhPDThcdGNSSH9?usp=sharing or scanning the QR code below.

Thank you for choosing "Ace Your California DMV Exam" as your study companion. Safe travels, and we hope you enjoy the open roads of California!

GLOSSARY

A

Account on the California DMV website (dmv.ca.gov): An online portal where individuals can manage DMV-related tasks such as scheduling exams, renewing licenses, and accessing personal DMV records.

Administrative Hearing: A legal proceeding where individuals can contest DMV decisions, such as license suspensions or revocations. It involves presenting evidence and witnesses.

Arrows: Indicate the direction of travel in lanes. Turn arrows show where you must turn, while straight arrows indicate where you must go straight. Follow the direction indicated by the arrows.

B

Behind-the-Wheel Drive Test: A practical driving test where applicants demonstrate their ability to operate a vehicle safely in real-world conditions, assessed by a DMV examiner.

Bike Lanes: Lanes designated for bicyclists only, typically marked by a single solid white line and signs, and sometimes painted bright green. It is illegal to drive in a bicycle lane unless parking (where permitted), entering or leaving the road, or turning (within 200 feet of an intersection).

Blind Intersection: An intersection where the driver's view is obstructed by trees, buildings, or other objects, making it difficult to see oncoming traffic.

Broken Yellow Line: A pavement marking indicating that passing is allowed if done safely when the broken line is next to your driving lane.

Business Districts: Areas typically characterized by commercial buildings and high pedestrian activity, where the speed limit is usually 25 mph unless otherwise posted.

C

Center Left Turn Lane: A lane in the middle of a two-way street, marked by two painted lines (inner broken and outer solid), used for preparing and making left turns or U-turns.

Class C Driver's License: A standard driver's license for operating regular passenger vehicles in California.

Commercial Driver's License (CDL): A special license required to operate commercial vehicles such as trucks and buses.

Construction Zones: Areas on the road where construction work is taking place, often marked by signs and reduced speed limits to ensure the safety of workers and drivers.

Crosswalk: A designated area for pedestrians to cross the road, marked with white or yellow lines.

Curb Markings:
- **Green Curb**: Allows for limited-time parking, as specified by signs or curb markings.
- **White Curb**: Indicates areas where you can stop only long enough to pick up or drop off passengers.
- **Yellow Curb**: Used for loading and unloading passengers or freight. Noncommercial vehicles are usually required to stay with the vehicle.
- **Blue Curb**: Reserved for disabled persons with a special placard or license plate.
- **Red Curb**: Indicates no stopping, standing, or parking.

D

Diamond-shaped Sign: Warning signs that alert drivers to special road conditions or potential dangers ahead.

Disabled Parking: Parking spaces reserved for individuals with disabilities, marked by a blue curb or sign, and requiring a special permit for use.

Double Solid White Lines: Pavement markings indicating a lane barrier between a regular use and a preferential use lane, such as a carpool lane. Lane changes are not permitted over these lines.

Double Solid Yellow Lines: Pavement markings indicating that passing is not allowed. Drivers must stay to the right of these lines unless in specific situations like entering a driveway.

E

Emergency (Parking) Brake: A brake used to keep a vehicle stationary when parked, also known as a handbrake or e-brake.

Exhaust Systems (Modified): Systems that have been altered to produce more noise or improve performance beyond legal limits. Increased penalties apply for violations.

F

Flashing Lights: Signals used by school buses, emergency vehicles, and at railroad crossings to indicate when you must stop.
  - **Yellow Flashing Lights on School Buses**: Indicate the bus is preparing to stop.
  - **Red Flashing Lights on School Buses**: Indicate you must stop until the lights stop flashing.
  - **Flashing Red Warning Lights at Railroad Crossings**: Indicate a train is approaching. You must stop and wait until the lights stop flashing, even if the gate rises.

Flashing Yellow Arrow: A traffic signal allowing left turns but requiring drivers to yield to oncoming traffic and pedestrians.

Fines and Double Fine Zones: Specific areas, often in work zones, where traffic violation fines are doubled due to increased collision-related injuries and fatalities.

G

Green Arrow: A traffic signal indicating that drivers have the right of way to make a protected turn in the direction of the arrow.

H

Hazard Lights: Flashing lights on a vehicle used to indicate a temporary stop, a breakdown, or a potential hazard to other drivers.

High Occupancy Vehicle (HOV) Lanes: Lanes reserved for vehicles with multiple passengers, buses, motorcycles, or low-emission vehicles with decals, indicated by a diamond symbol.

I

Intersections: Places where two or more roads meet, with specific rules for navigating based on traffic signals and signs.

L

Lane Markings: Pavement markings that guide the movement of traffic and indicate where drivers should position their vehicles.

Learner's Permit: A permit allowing individuals, usually teens, to practice driving under the supervision of a licensed adult before obtaining a full driver's license.

License Suspension: The temporary removal of a person's driving privileges due to violations or unsafe driving practices.

M

Medical Conditions: Health issues that could affect driving abilities, requiring documentation and possibly additional testing for a driver's license.

Move Over Law: Requires drivers to move over a lane or slow down when approaching stopped emergency or waste service vehicles displaying flashing lights.

N

No Parking Zones: Areas where parking is prohibited to maintain safety and accessibility, often marked by signs or red curbs.

O

Obstructing Windows: The act of placing signs or objects on a vehicle's windows that block the driver's view, which is illegal.

P

Parking on Hills: Specific parking techniques used to prevent a vehicle from rolling when parked on an incline.

Passing Lanes: Designated lanes on a multi-lane road, typically the far-left lane, used specifically for overtaking slower vehicles safely.

Pedestrian Push Button: A button that pedestrians press to activate the WALK signal at intersections.

Pedestrian Signals: Indicators for pedestrians to walk or wait.

- **WALK or Walking Person**: Indicates it is safe to cross the street.
- **DON'T WALK or Raised Hand**: Signals that crossing is not allowed. Pedestrians should not enter the crosswalk.

Planned Non-Operation (PNO): Status you can file for if your vehicle will not be operated or parked on public roads, to avoid paying full registration fees.

Pre-Drive Inspection: A check performed before the behind-the-wheel test to ensure the vehicle meets safety standards.

Painted Messages:

- **Yield Lines**: Rows of small triangles extending across the lane, indicating where you should yield to oncoming traffic or pedestrians, often found at roundabouts and mid-block crosswalks.
- **Sharrows (Shared Lane Markings)**: Indicate lanes shared between bicyclists and motorists. Consist of a bike symbol with two chevrons above it.

R

Railroad Crossing Sign: A sign indicating the presence of railroad tracks ahead, requiring drivers to look and listen for trains and be prepared to stop.

Rearview Mirrors: Mirrors that allow the driver to see behind the vehicle, required for safe driving.

Red Arrow: A traffic signal indicating that turning in the direction of the arrow is prohibited.

Rear-facing Child Passenger Restraint System: A safety seat designed to face the rear of the vehicle, required for children under 2 years old, under 40 pounds, and under 3 feet 4 inches tall.

Reflective Markings: Enhance the visibility of lane markings, especially at night and in poor weather conditions. Different colors indicate different types of markings:

- **White Reflectors**: Used to mark lane lines or the right edge of the roadway.
- **Yellow Reflectors**: Mark the left edge of the roadway on divided highways and one-way streets.
- **Red Reflectors**: Indicate areas not to be entered or used, such as the wrong side of a divided highway.
  - **Right-of-Way**: Rules determining which vehicle or pedestrian has the priority in different traffic situations to prevent accidents and ensure smooth traffic flow.

S

School Zones: Areas near schools with reduced speed limits to protect children, often marked by signs and flashing lights.

Senior Drivers: Drivers who are 70 years old or older, with specific renewal processes and recommendations to ensure safe driving.

Solid Green Light: A traffic signal indicating it is safe to proceed but requiring drivers to yield to any vehicles, bicyclists, or pedestrians still in the intersection.

Special Speed Limits: Speed limits set for specific areas or conditions, such as school zones, construction zones, and blind intersections.

Safety Zones: Areas marked by raised buttons or markers where pedestrians wait for buses, streetcars, and trolleys. Do not drive through a safety zone.

Sharrows (Shared Lane Markings): Indicate lanes shared between bicyclists and motorists. Consist of a bike symbol with two chevrons above it.

Side Airbags: Airbags located on the sides of the vehicle, which children should not sit next to for safety reasons.

Sobriety Tests: Tests administered by law enforcement to determine if a driver is under the influence of alcohol or drugs. Refusing these tests can result in immediate license suspension.

T

T-intersections: Intersections where one road ends and meets another road at a right angle, with specific right-of-way rules.

Temporary Operating Permit (TOP): Permit that allows you to legally drive if your registration has expired and you are unable to complete the renewal process immediately.

Traffic Violator School: An educational course for drivers who have committed a traffic violation, allowing them to keep the citation off their insurance record.

Turn Signals: Lights on a vehicle that indicate the driver's intention to turn or change lanes.

- **Left Turn**: Extend your left arm horizontally.

- **Right Turn**: Extend your left arm with elbow bent upward.
- **Stopping or Slowing Down**: Extend your left arm downward.

U

U-turn: A maneuver to turn the vehicle around to go in the opposite direction.

Unattended Children and Pets: Never leave children or pets unattended in a vehicle, especially in hot weather, due to the risk of heatstroke and death.

V

Vision Test: A test to ensure a driver can see well enough to drive safely, often required when applying for or renewing a driver's license.

Visibility for Bicyclists at Night: Crucial for safety, requiring the following equipment:
- **Front Lamp**: A white light visible from 300 feet.
- **Rear Red Reflector or Light**: Visible from 500 feet.
- **Pedal Reflectors**: White or yellow reflectors on each pedal, shoes, or ankles, visible from 200 feet.
- **Wheel Reflectors**: White or yellow reflectors on the front wheel and a white or red reflector on the rear wheel, or reflectorized tires.

W

Windshield: The front window of a vehicle, which must provide a clear, unobstructed view for the driver and examiner during the driving test.

Work Zones: Areas where roadwork is being done, often marked by signs and reduced speed limits to ensure the safety of workers and drivers.

Made in the USA
Las Vegas, NV
05 March 2025